How to Win Arguments

How to Win Arguments and Refute Misleading Logic

(Essential Tactics of Logic and Persuasion to Win in Your Career and Relationships)

Joseph Reed

Published By **Bengion Cosalas**

Joseph Reed

All Rights Reserved

How to Win Arguments: How to Win Arguments and Refute Misleading Logic (Essential Tactics of Logic and Persuasion to Win in Your Career and Relationships)

ISBN 978-1-7774976-7-5

No part of this guidebook shall be reproduced in any form without permission in writing from the publisher except in the case of brief quotations embodied in critical articles or reviews.

Legal & Disclaimer

The information contained in this book is not designed to replace or take the place of any form of medicine or professional medical advice. The information in this book has been provided for educational & entertainment purposes only.

The information contained in this book has been compiled from sources deemed reliable, and it is accurate to the best of the Author's knowledge; however, the Author cannot guarantee its accuracy and validity and cannot be held liable for any errors or omissions. Changes are periodically made to this book. You must consult your doctor or get professional medical advice before using any of the suggested remedies, techniques, or information in this book.

Upon using the information contained in this book, you agree to hold harmless the Author from and against any damages, costs, and expenses, including any legal fees potentially resulting from the application of any of the information provided by this guide. This disclaimer applies to any damages or injury caused by the use and application, whether directly or indirectly, of any advice or information presented, whether for breach of contract, tort, negligence, personal injury, criminal intent, or under any other cause of action.

You agree to accept all risks of using the information presented inside this book. You need to consult a professional medical practitioner in order to ensure you are both able and healthy enough to participate in this program.

Table Of Contents

Chapter 1: Understand The Basics 1

Chapter 2: Understand Your Opponent . 10

Chapter 3: Level Mindedness 21

Chapter 4: Be Logical 30

Chapter 5: Overview Of The Word 'Argument' 59

Chapter 6: Constructing A Logical Argument 64

Chapter 7: Why Do We Feel The Need Of An Arguement? 67

Chapter 8: Why Your Arguments Fail? ... 71

Chapter 9: How To Win Any Argument .. 79

Chapter 10: The Biggest Enemy To Decisions 92

Chapter 11: Keep Your Options Open .. 101

Chapter 12: No Decision Is Still A Decision 115

Chapter 13: Testing Your Choices 120

Chapter 14: Take The Three Ps............ 131

Chapter 15: Get Ready To Make A Wrong Decision 141

Chapter 16: Take A Stand..................... 154

Chapter 17: Don't Beat Around The Bush 165

Chapter 18: Be The Change.................. 178

Chapter 1: Understand The Basics

Less Offense

Maybe the maximum imperative issue to consider whilst you land up in an problem is to by no means attack the opportunity man or woman. Else, you could see them final down and declining to pay attention to some thing you need to mention. When this takes place you can't win. Not seeming like you're a raving neurotic calls for a quiet air of mystery and a peaceful mind-set.

Whenever you are eager and obsessed on your function, you have to keep up manage of your feelings. On the off threat that you lose your mood, you or all gatherings included will lose. Some a part of staying quiet is knowing a way to cope with your emotions.

Never assault your rival. In the event that you say some thing out of indignation, your phrases can in no manner be taken returned. This will damage your present argument, further to your destiny circle of relatives individuals with this individual.

You can in no way take once more terms, so dependably anticipate in advance than you talk. You can, in any case, correctly avoid verbal assaults. This implies you come back terms back to the subsequent individual while retaining manipulate of your emotions.

For example, in case you're in a store and any person gets to be angry in mild of the truth which you took the final maximum amazing modern-day day toy for Christmas off the rack, in place of hollering, "That is Mine!" you will just divert it once more to them.

You may additionally additionally say as an opportunity, "I understand you're dissatisfied which you did now not get this toy for your little one. In any case, do you clearly do not forget that trying to push me out of the manner is becoming conduct?"

If you avoid damaging comments and practices with out attending to be furious, the alternative character turns into exhausted of the Argument or widely recognized they had been being absurd and yield. It's important to maintain your emotions ordinary and pay interest absolutely on the opposite person's emotions.

Rather than announcing, "I'm livid!" you may turn it around on them via manner of manner of supplying, "You look like irate." If they solution that you're being endorse, do no longer concede or deny a few aspect. Simply answer, "Now, why do you don't forget that?" The robust point of avoidance isn't about copying the alternative individual; it is about compelling them to apprehend and take control of their emotions.

Avoiding terrible feelings is a totally possible technique to win an trouble.

Know the Winning Side

Despite the reality that the easy demonstration of diverting the argument can get you a achievement, there are wonderful processes to viably win, for example, selecting the a success difficulty will assure you a triumph always. This may also seem like a misleadingly clean stride, but there are a few levels because it's to a first rate amount about understanding a way to choose your fights.

We ought to take a gander at times: one political and one in the domestic.

Amid the start of america, slavery became a polarizing trouble that in the long run dove it into civil battle. At the time, numerous human beings had strong convictions on each sides of the verbal warfare of words.

Some Thinkers depended on that moral brilliant grow to be advancing and servitude might be nullified eventually. In this way, by manner of way of standing organization closer to it they picked the effective facet.

The individuals who battled to hold bondage couldn't have obtained no matter how strong their Arguments, basically thinking about that subjection modified into ethically, socially, and morally off-base.

Look at example ; say you've got were given a five-one year-antique who watches you play your guitar. One day they inquire as to whether or not or no longer they are capable of play it and your feature reflex is to say no. Yet, do not forget the effects of turning them down. Likely you will argue, you could each get agitated, the minute can remodel into tears and damage sentiments, and the day may be destroyed.

In any case, at the off chance that you pick out out out the powerful thing you will postpone, consider their solicitation, and in some time answer, "Yes, you could play my guitar at the off threat that you sit down down via me and permit me help you." Through that certifiable proclamation you train your tyke to deal with the guitar, and that you'll be their train which expands the bond amongst you.

An Argument (or healthful of rage) modified into have become away on the grounds that you picked your fight and picked the high quality component. This have to now not endorse that you want to dependably offer into your teen.

Yet rather to suggest which you provide things enough perception, and select in case your reflexive reaction is the most becoming for the situation. Picking the effective element isn't normally clean as you want time to don't forget the great factors of the Argument.

At that factor you need to undergo in thoughts the confirmation in backing of each thing, and maintain in mind which seems to have a more grounded characteristic or this is within the ethical right.

Don't be Loose with Your Words

You can clearly win an hassle in the event that you have a decent one in any case. To placed it evidently, you need to listen what you are announcing.

Like a group debater planning for an up and coming argument, you have to study the situation absolutely. Be set up to decrease again your function with precisely investigated realities and insights.

Bear it in your thoughts, to inquire about the contradicting argument as a exquisite detail of your approach. Completely dismember your non-public argument from begin to complete. Make best you've got robust supporting focuses, case from your and evidence from professionals at the issue you'll be Arguing.

Comprehend the argument in contrary and ahead, and be prepared to react to inquiries and counterpoints which could sucker punch you if you're not readied.

Never walk into a hassle little approximately. As you painstakingly extend your Argument, the requirements within the decrease lower back of the "Guideline of Three" are an incredible technique to make a balanced role. This idea gadgets that things are nice even as they come in threes (Three Blind mice, three little pigs; "pals, Romans, Countrymen"; "Life, Liberty, and the Pursuit of Happiness").

Arguments often spring up all of sudden. There modified into no possibility to manufacture a guns keep of cloth to bolster your angle. When someone says some thing you enjoy compelled to argue, prevent, and take a deep breath earlier than you open your mouth.

While in brief brooding about the situation, you could do without a doubt one in every of four possibilities to postpone the argument until you've give you your technique:

1.You may additionally need to recommend the person who you have to recollect it and resume the dialogue in a while.

2.You can anticipate a announcement of worried consciousness, showing which you're giving their Argument and your response due belief.

3.You can take delivery of a scrutinizing outward look and maintain up your pointer in a "supply me a minute" movement and however genuinely say, "I require a minute please. You've given me a high-quality deal to maintain in thoughts."

4.If a trouble is coming, set a few up top notch focuses in advance of time.

Chapter 2: Understand Your Opponent

Know Your Enemy

When you understand both the man or woman and their Argument, you location yourself in a advanced role to make improvement. "Knowing your rival" implies you understand who they will be as someone.

You realise what drives them, what awes them, and what fears they have got, for with this information you can define your Arguments in a way that speaks to what is essential to this person.

You can have interaction their feeling of morals, their power approximately diligent work, their commitment to motives, et cetera. When you understand your rival, you likewise discover approximately the focuses in their Argument you can need to venture.

Knowing your rival likewise helps you to distinguish feeble and strong focuses on your personal argument so you can build up a important association earlier than your adversary can assault.

When you recognize your adversary's facet of the volume headed dialogue – at the same time as you're taking a really perfect opportunity to scrutinize the focuses that backing their Argument – you're better prepared to stand off concerning the ones focuses or to elevate some distance superior ones helping the facet of your argument.

Reading Body Language

You'll must recognize that the opportunity individual is prepared what they are pronouncing, further to how they may be saying it.

There are severa signs and signs that may be definitely smooth to peruse. Individuals show what they're thoroughly thinking about their stance, hand motions, pores and pores and pores and skin shading and respiration. You can make use of the ones non-verbal portions of statistics to discern out what any individual way, or how they enjoy about you are mentioning. This statistics may be useful amid an amicable or non-accommodating open deliberation.

Individuals normally have a tendency to fall into one or a greater amount of three commands: Visual, emotional or auditory thinkers. On the off risk that you recognize how someone thinks, you could display your argument all of the extra correctly.

Additionally, you can have to determine out how to mention matters so the possibility individual short comprehends what you are trying to skip on.

Visual thinkers envision the area in snap shots. They have a tendency to speak rapidly in a shrill voice because the pictures fly thru their head, and show stress of their neck and shoulders after they get to be enlivened.

They frequently deliver in seen phrases, as an example, the situation makes them blue, otherwise you can't see their thoughts-set. To viably speak with those individuals, you need to likewise make use of visible dialect.

Auditory thinkers suppose in sounds. These human beings frequently make little, musical inclinations after they communicate, or tilt their head in particular to the side just as tuning in. They furthermore utilize terms like "The entryway is absolutely squeaky," or "You aren't tuning in. Possibly I in reality have to expose up the amount." To effectively talk with those people, you ought to utilize sound-related dialect.

Emotional thinkers particular via feelings. These people will be inclined to inhale profoundly and speak in a mild, conscious voice with their head tilted quite. They employ emotional phrases, for instance, "I revel in this", or "you're making me furious."

To viably speak with the ones human beings, you ought to utilize passionate dialect, as an instance, quiet, unwind, peace, amicability, peacefulness, liberal, kind, acclaim, retaining, having a place, and so on.

When you notice how a person else conveys, it is less tough to get your mind crosswise over to them all at once and impact them in your attitude. You can likewise spark off them through non-verbal communication with the aid of reflecting their sports activities.

If they are being outlandish and disturbed, you can impersonate their function. In the occasion that they stand, you stand. In the event that they fold their hands, you fold your hands, and so on. Try no longer to do it , satirically, or within the period in-between.

You ought to regulate your self to them bodily, which indicates status or sitting along with your shoulders rectangular closer to them, your head held rectangular on so your eyes meet theirs. Look certain, quiet, unemotional but associated. You want them to understand you are being attentive to their side of the Argument and are considering them critical. Individuals with a combat outlook are organized to address their rival on the playing concern. Be that as it is able to, this on the spot technique can swiftly diffuse their bodily indignation.

On the off hazard that this does not artwork you could strive a "loosen up" signal to represent they ought to unwind. Spread out your palms, hands confronting down approximately waist excessive sincerely as you are tenderly pushing them down. Keep up eye contact and a quiet manner. Do it unobtrusively so it's far scarcely taken be aware.

Practice Agreeing

Before you could win an trouble, you and the alternative man or woman want to be at the identical internet net web page. Correspondence is a -way put together that involves the cooperation of tuning in, reacting, and selecting choices contemplating what's listened. In the occasion that there is concordance in the correspondence, neither one of the activities considers winning as they have got lengthy long gone to a shared comprehension. Obviously, you are in charge of your aspect of the situation. The great exercise is to invite more questions.

Build Rapport

How approximately we now take a gander at how you could make use of non-verbal verbal exchange to build up outstanding affinity to enlarge your opportunities of winning an Argument. Affinity is the problem that takes region while human beings are in a country of concord, or are at the same wavelength and relate well to each other.

Individuals who have affinity see every special, listen every out extraordinary, and fulfill some thing regardless of the opportunity that it's miles equitable to grow to be extra familiar with every other better.

People with extremely good compatibility often advocate it thru reflecting each wonderful's non-verbal verbal exchange - along side stance and eye touch - and frequently employ the same manner of speaking and phrases. Individuals who effectively win Arguments make affinity that advances believe.

Reflecting or coordinating the alternative person isn't always much like imitating; it is extra similar to being at their degree. Coordinating eye touch and voice-to-voice is a crucial piece of installing region affinity. Amid the system of creating compatibility you do not need to concur with the alternative character.

In any case, you do want to widely known what they are affirming, and that you regard their attitude. You can do this through using using a way of speakme that suggests sympathy and comprehension. What's extra, with excessive best non-verbal communique that indicates you are exactly thinking about what they'll be declaring.

You can likewise do it with the choice of your terms. For example, "but" is a horrible conjunction a amazing manner to damage affinity. By announcing, "Yes, I pay interest you. Be that as it could, " you will located an surrender to constructing affinity. Rather, you ought to utilize a first rate conjunction, as an instance, "and."

How would probable you sense at the off hazard which you have a look at, "I listen what you are stating, but I think numerous stuff."? You probable experience emptied and ignored. Presently on the equal time as you examine, "I heard what you stated, and I enjoy that is an brilliant concept," it has a notably more terrific tone no matter the reality that one-of-a-kind 3 letters have changed. You may moreover even make compatibility with individuals you do now not take care of.

Consider it assembly them somewhere amongst building an extension to possible correspondence. In case you are conveying efficaciously, then you can each paintings in the direction of a palatable self-discipline in your Argument.

When you have superb affinity with a person, they may probable truely be aware of your issues and be conscious of what you supply to the table.

Out-Smart Your Opponent

As became expressed within the important tip, you want to in no manner assault your adversary verbally or bodily. You can, anyways, intelligently examine their argument and make use of any omission in reason on your gain.

Amid your Argument you want to take benefit of any blunder, deceiving mind, or slip in judgments your adversary makes. When you find out an imperfection, you will want to counter it with certainties that backing your feature

When you've got were given strong realities to counter enthusiastic or wrong Arguments, you are taking every one of the tooth out of your rival's chomp. When alert: If your Argument is a diploma headed communicate on a particular subject matter, then calling interest to shortcomings and mistakes to your adversary's Argument is an top notch machine to illustrate your function is proper.

However, if you will likely win the Argument without stressful or genuinely worrying the other man or woman, then this can be a test for the cause that humans usually get agitated even as they will be informed or confirmed they may be incorrect.

The idea proper right here is to supply your remarks with apprehend and belief for the individual. Back to the uncle: Obviously he administers to his nephew, Bob, or he would not be

Chapter 3: Level Mindedness

"Argument" often invokes a picture of issue. While a trouble does no longer want to bring about such terrific emotions, it is able to be fantastically enthusiastic and can turn into an unstable assembly which at very last annihilations the aftereffect of a amazing result. Regardless of the opportunity that you discern out a way to stay even tempered and realistic, the possibility person's emotions can bubble and the argument takes a horrific turn.

Along the ones lines, in the interim you're controlling your own precise conceivably horrible and vain emotions, you're soothing those same emotions in your adversary. You have to have in thoughts so as no longer to pass on that you are disparaging or trying to manage the person. Your sports need to be surprisingly inconspicuous and quieting. Another approach to diffuse outrage is to say no to wind up furious your self.

Numerous people count on that it's hard to be unfavourable in the direction of any man or woman who is quiet. On the off hazard that a person is unsettled, with the resource of retaining your voice low and do not react with displeasure or countering, they may reflect your sports and cool down. Utilizing your voice delicately is a few different method to diffuse outrage or constrain a person to pay interest all the greater almost.

Like creatures, people can enjoy or even be aware fear and could assault substantially all the extra fiercely. Be quiet, keep your voice low and level like an night time radio show host, allow your frame to unwind, and inhale little by little and equitably in advance than talking. Another approach to quiet any person who is getting disturbed up is thru handling them together with your non-verbal conversation.

In the occasion that the person you are arguing with receives to be irate, you will need to coordinate their characteristic, behavior, and voice. Generally, you are dialing their emotions down various or . On the off hazard that they stand, fold their palms and talk boisterously. At that thing you stand, fold your fingers, and talk multiple decibels a good buy lots less uproariously.

You hold pacing them beforehand and backward to installation a musicality to area you both on the identical enthusiastic diploma of affinity. Without them understanding it, you are riding them to your favored give up end result. As you lead them proper right into a quieter state, they'll take after your lead and display contemplated behavior. You'll deliver down the pitch of your voice, unfurl your arms, and cope with a greater informal physical appearance. Gradually unwind your shoulders, your face, and through the span of a few minutes flow into something remains of your frame into an exceptionally informal, consonant position. On the off hazard which you pick out, you may grin warmly. You'll be surprised at how the other man or woman takes after your lead proper right into a quiet, non-indignant state, and may neglect what you had been arguing about.

Diffuse Your Own Anger – Take A Time Out

Obviously, diffusing our private specific displeasure can be tough to do mentally even as your emotions are going for walks excessive. In a few instances, the quality way to diffuse outrage efficaciously is to step an prolonged manner from the state of affairs for a minute, to take a duration out.

Things being what they may be, we see the "day out" accomplished viably as part of an collection of settings. A compelling day ride in video games can be a beneficial device to "ice" the adversary, who may moreover furthermore have been have had a further of positive stress on their side, moreover to offer a highbrow and bodily breather for the enterprise business enterprise who wants to reset and recover their thoughts to a remarkable united states of america of america.

Great guardians likewise employ the day journey, each for themselves and their youngsters. The day trip is most correctly carried out even as a teenager is displaying poor enthusiastic conduct, as an example; oppositeness, animosity, rowdiness, sassing and so on.

With the day journey the tyke is expelled from what has modified proper into a strained or unpleasant condition, vicinity by myself in a corner or in their place to chill out, and in a while usual to rejoin the gathering or condition once their feelings are once more below manipulate. Obviously, the day ride fills in too on guardians because it does on kids. An astute figure realizes that once they get to be irate with their teen it is wonderful for them to undertaking back and experience a reprieve; no argument can be received, and no first rate can come, from speaking with a person else even as you're vexed and passionate.

By playing a reprieve, a parent can clear their head, think all the greater legitimately, and be better prepared to speak with their youngster. The truth of the matter is that after our feelings get to be uplifted, whilst indignation units in, we lose our functionality to legitimately reason.

Accordingly, proper right here and there the high-quality way to transport beyond an deadlock in belligerence that became come to due to indignation is to take a duration out. By venturing a long way from the condition and taking a few minutes all by myself to take a seat down back down you could maneuver your feelings into take a look at, refocus in your identifying objective, and reappear the argument as a superior communicator.

Take a Time Out

You can move for an afternoon trip quietly, via genuinely venturing decrease back for a 2nd and taking a full breath seeking to clean your brain. On the other hand, you could authoritatively ask for a duration out, essentially announcing, "I require a minute please" and venturing without prevent. On the off chance that practicable, at the same time as casting off a period out pass from the character you're arguing with, probable venturing over to three domestic windows. You have to select now not to exacerbate the state of affairs thru searching as if you are gambling Judas on a person, it is surprisingly discourteous non-verbal communication. However, you need a minute for protection. Thus, at the off hazard that you turn your decrease lower back at the grounds that you are searching out a window or at a fish aquarium, you could get your place with out seeming rude. After a minute, essentially re-technique the possibility character (on the off risk that they seem like organized) and, in a quiet voice, rejoin the speak.

Use Your Emotions

Sensibly you understand that shouting at your infant to give up crying isn't going to purpose them to stop. Be that as it may, as your thoughts shouts from all the commotion, you find out it nearly not possible no longer to holler. Rationale evaluations trouble defeating this diploma of disappointment as there are enthusiastic and bodily responses covered.

You're no longer shouting at the infant; you're hollering on the commotion and what it's doing on your rational soundness. In this way, people are pushed via feeling, and you can make use of that information to win your arguments. Sensibly arguments want to be bolstered by means of truths and approach of reasoning. Be that as it could, at the off danger that you have an opportunity to earnings by way of way of the use of your rival's emotions, there may be no cause now not to do it.

You can likewise employ emotions to verify essential argument, and discover shared conviction as said already. Let's assume you are arguing with any man or woman at the university board about your youngster's university protection. You can quiet matters through beginning with a harmless, non-debilitating inquiry severa humans may have on the main edge of their mind. For example, you may ask, "Don't you concur that we need to address how we are able to make our kids more steady?" When the alternative party has the same opinion, you may employ this little triumph as a springboard for further discourse.

Chapter 4: Be Logical

Arguments are every now and then gained on feeling. The great debaters understand how to utilize cause to bolster their function and subliminally compel the opportunity individual to consent to their function.

How you form your argument is a piece of usually showing an problem. While introducing your component and trying to persuade somebody to concur with you, you need to make it smooth for them to take after your reasoning. Leave a route of crumbs to transport them into your even though gadget. In discourse there can be a platitude which you want to enlighten your crowd what you're concerning to permit them to comprehend, then allow them to understand, and in a while permit them to recognize what you truely permit them to understand.

This holds similarly legitimate for belligerence. As a case, you had your car towed to the dealership because it might now not begin. The workman says your battery is vain and the assure has terminated. You argue this may no longer be the state of affairs for the cause that they supplanted your battery actually thirteen months decrease again. They say they're sad, yet this is first-rate the manner it is. So you pardon your self and you begin to type the events out.

You understand that soon once they supplanted the battery the primary run through the car lighting started out out to decrease and weird topics had been taking place electrically. You took the car again in and the workman determined an lousy circuit board that changed into bringing on the breakdowns. Presently best multiple months after the fact you've got have been given every other dead battery and enjoy the 2 times can be associated.

In the event that you had hollered on the repairman and allow him understand they had been convicts, that that they had in reality say that wasn't their hassle, your battery modified into no more under guarantee, and this is the cease of that. However, on the off chance that you control your feelings and sensibly type out your argument, you could have a advanced hazard for a strength of mind.

Begin thru grade by grade restating the difficulty and that you are feeling there is probably a larger problem. At that aspect address motivating them to look your facet. Remind the repairman this is your 2nd battery; and that the primary became bitter in truth earlier than your circuit board went haywire. Inquire as to whether or not or not or no longer he those occurrences might have been related, and in the event that it is possible the horrible circuit board harmed the number one battery. In the occasion that he has the same opinion that is workable, then pass earlier to make clear that likely this battery may also moreover have been harmed too and will likewise have abbreviated the battery's lifestyles. Request that he recall those possible consequences with the control director, and to reexamine whether or not the battery have to supplant at no price.

Obviously, the outcomes have to cross in any case. Be that as it is able to, by using way of the use of sensibly associating all the specks you advanced the possibilities of him seeing your attitude and that you could win your argument.

Covert Losses in Wins

Regularly it's far believed that a concept is correct or wrong, a few aspect is tremendous or pessimistic, a person has received or misplaced. In any case, no longer all that subjects in life is good sized as there may be that little little little bit of fact some location inside the center. At times triumphing isn't always what's crucial. Once in a while a stop end result cannot be modified or an decent end be come to.

In any case, with the right u . S . Of thoughts even an apparent misfortune may be visible as a fractional win. It is in truth all in mild of popularity. In a few times, you can participate in an problem for which there seems to be no preference. Neither one of the factors has suitable sufficient certainties to steer their adversary, and could live relentless to their underlying argument. In any case, with the aid of manner of reframing the scenario, they every turn out as victors and now not disasters.

Another desire is to find out shared opinion and arrange a tradeoff. Keep in mind that in a combat each components get beat up. Yet, in a good buy every components win.

Show Some Gracefulness

Ordinarily you'll take part in an trouble with human beings close to you. The concept of belligerence calls for a few stage of considering the result, which thusly requires a few form of affiliation along with your adversary.

While you can at times argue with outsiders - perhaps a discourteous man or woman at the auto wash, or a pushy vehicle salesperson – you argue all of the more regularly with the ones near you, for example, companions, family, and pals. Winning an trouble isn't generally the most essential end result to make improvement in the direction of. You need to win with out harming connections, that could damage your feature in future arguments.

It can come to be an infinite loop wherein you will wind up losing an lousy lot greater than you win. Try no longer to be a ruined recreation. By being an agile victor you may limit damage emotions, and invite future contradictions and a fantastic spherical of stopping. The maximum exceptional technique to win an problem is to supply the opportunity character over on your mind-set, encourage them to appearance your facet this is upheld with motive and actualities, and to concede they have been now not right. The remarkable end result for you, manifestly, is that your function is the right one.

In the occasion which you get a beneficiant quiet submission from your accomplice, do no longer brag. Be joyful that the each of you settled on the first rate choice collectively, and be beneficiant about it. Tell them which you understand why they deviated, but that you're satisfied they were sufficiently open to apprehend your solution modified into the splendid method. In the event which you brag and make them revel in idiotic, they might not will to concede destiny mistakes stimulated through a paranoid worry of being criticized. Play it cool, be smooth, and make sure.

Whenever you land up in a hassle with the equal character, you may curve and allow them to have their very own specific way. In the occasion that you are adaptable each on occasion and don't deliver your feel of proper and wrong a threat to act as a burden, you may see them extra liable to twist moreover.

When you have got given and cope with each components, in reality all people is a champ!

Don'ts

Taking after the progressions underneath will pretty decorate your arguing effects and avoid smooth arguing pitfalls:

• You cannot win with the useful resource of injuring absolutely everyone's emotions. Regardless of the opportunity that their certainties are not right, their emotions are valid and now not up to talk. You need to be legit in your feelings, and you need to do likewise to your rival.

• Don't employ unverified purpose to help your sentiments.

• Don't supply down your self to childishness.

• Don't argue most effective for belligerence

• Don't intrude with others on the identical time as they're showing their case.

• Don't communicate in uncertain phrases, as an example, want to, might, need to or may. Additionally, avoid ambiguous solutions, as an example, "Numerous humans say" or "Commentators have asserted" or "Research seems," till you can substantiate them with proof or refers to.

• Don't argue at the same time as you comprehend you are incorrect as all of us isn't proper at instances.

Stop Arguing, Start Having Discussions

This possibly appears counterintuitive but the superb way to address an problem is sincerely no longer to argue. By don't argue, I mean avoid a verbal conflict at all expenses. Don't pass in to a dialogue with the idea that the opportunity side of the argument have to see that you are proper no matter what. Come to the desk, so to talk, geared up to have an honest, civil talk with others. Try to get beyond the concept of "winning" or "dropping" an difficulty. Start seeing your conversational companion as a clearly that, a partner. You are companions on a search for fact collectively, not adversaries.

Be Prepared To Change Your Mind

Being willing to have an honest communique technique be willing to trade your thoughts. The hassle with seeing discussions/arguments in best win/lose phrases is that it means that if you look at, you lose. If your talk accomplice shows you that your reasoning or evidence is defective, you have a danger to research some thing. Yet you received't study a few element if you think that having your argument be defeated is losing, or a few thing you need to be ashamed about.

Define Your Terms

The fact seeker Voltaire said "If you choice to speak with me, first outline your phrases." This is sound recommendation. Have you ever been in a scenario in which it appeared which includes you were disagreeing with a person, but they have been definitely simply using a word in another way than you used it? This takes place all the time, so it is very crucial to define your terms. Start out thru announcing "When I say This I imply Precise Definition." It could probably appear to be a ache to need to try this, but it will save you some of time in the long run thru not arguing with someone over definitions. At the outset of the conversation, avoid misunderstandings with the aid of defining your terms.

Really Listen

So regularly it takes area that as people talk to us we aren't in fact listening. Instead we're deliberating what we're going to say in response, otherwise considering some element irrelevant like what we're going to have for lunch. Really attempt to be present within the verbal exchange, pay interest in your partner and supply them your complete hobby. If you don't concentrate to them you threat false impression them, growing useless confusion. Furthermore, how are you going to steer someone of an opportunity angle in case you don't honestly understand the view they preserve? Active listening will make you higher at persuasion, reduce confusion, and it's far simply courteous except.

Re-specific Or Rephrase Their Position

As quick as you've heard a person's function on something, you're probable already thinking about strategies to dismantle their argument and prove your self correct. Stop. Don't try this. Instead, take a moment to virtually digest their argument and then repeat it lower back to them as you recognize it. The truth seeker Daniel Dennett recommends that you try and rephrase it in a manner this is so clear and concise that they are saying "Wow, I want I'd notion of setting it like that!" Why? Because this enables make sure each elements of the argument are at the identical net web page. We've all had instances wherein we've had to say "That's no longer what I'm saying the least bit! What I advise is..." Don't do that to different humans. Instead, make certain you truly apprehend the aspect they're making in advance than urgent on. This will save you time since you received't get slowed down in misunderstandings, and will earn you factors alongside aspect your interlocutor (conversational accomplice) by way of the usage of displaying them you were in reality listening to them.

Remember The Things You Agree About

Don't attention on only your disagreements. Remember to consciousness on the property you settle approximately as properly. Taking a second to focus on what you compromise about will help reassure the alternative facet of the argument which you aren't seeking to be purposefully opposed or obstinate. It can decorate how receptive they're for your argument thru engendering correct will, and could set a extra civil tone for the conversation going in advance.

Understand Them, Get Into Their Head

We often fail to steer others due to the fact we consciousness on what convinces us and then push that reasoning onto them. We take the motives we've got for a perception (or the motives we inform ourselves we've got), and then assume that those reasons will convince the other character. Yet your talk accomplice isn't you. They think differently and characteristic splendid values. If you want to persuade them you may need to apprehend them. Try to recognize their ideals, values and concept manner. Ask your self what ought to convince you when you have been them. You want to tailor your argument everyday with their worldview if you want to be persuasive.

Understand Yourself, Ask What Your Goal Is

Take a second earlier than you start an trouble to ask your self what your goals are. If you don't have easy motives for trying a few thing, how do you count on to speak those motives to anyone else? Ask yourself what you want out of this verbal exchange, consider the problem you have and what steps will want to be taken to solve it. If your companion in no manner lets in by way of the usage of doing chores across the house, then your reason is to steer them that they've to assist. When you understand that the shortage of help with chores motives you frustration, you can them speak that frustration on your associate.

Wait Until You Are Calm To Begin

Don't rush into an issue complete of anger, this may set a horrible tone right off the bat and make it extra difficult to persuade your associate of your characteristic. Wait until some of the warmth has surpassed earlier than beginning a communicate with someone, it's critical to start out at the right foot.

Pick Your Battles

Figure out which arguments actually need available. If you try to argue about each last little perceived moderate or injustice, it'll in all likelihood be seen as commonplace for you voice dissent. Your phrases will then have lots less effect even as you do improve an critical trouble, and past that no individual likes someone who is continuously horrible. Constantly stopping will stress you out too, manifestly.

"I'd a amazing deal as an alternative have 15 people arguing about some thing than 15 human beings splitting into camps, each aspect glad it is proper and no longer talking to the opposite."

 -- Linus Torvalds

Stay Calm During The Discussion

Do you need being yelled at? No, hardly ever absolutely everyone does. If you enjoy the urge to start yelling and screaming, kick back out and stroll some distance from the argument for a piece. Take deep breaths if you sense yourself begin to get agitated, persevering with a communicate with anger will handiest make matters worse.

Don't Insult

This is this kind of ones that looks as if common revel in, but many human beings though need to be reminded of it. Don't inn to mockery or insults. For one, insults don't offer any actual reasons or proof, in order that they aren't going to be effective if your purpose is to persuade a person of your perspective. In fact, quite the alternative will take region. Insults usually have a tendency to make people greater shielding and that they make you appearance immature, growing the danger that your arguments will honestly be unnoticed.

But Do Make It Personal

You shouldn't get non-public with the useful resource of insulting a person, but you may get personal through private anecdotes. Telling a non-public story on your accomplice with evocative pics and phrases can open them as a lot as persuasion. Crafting a tale that appeals to their feel of empathy or compassion can be a completely powerful tactic. Take phrase despite the fact that that a private narrative shouldn't be your only argument. A private tale can paint a image of the scenario, but you may need to lower again it up with actual evidence and sound reasoning.

Don't Open Old Wounds

If a beyond argument modified into settled don't circulate bringing it up inside the present day-day one. It's an useless distraction from the hassle reachable. In addition, it isn't sincere to carry up vintage errors or accidents your interlocutor has made to attempt to undermine their credibility. How may want to you enjoy if on every occasion you attempted to make a detail about some thing it was omitted due to the reality you have been incorrect once earlier than? Keep the point of interest at the trouble handy and look at the current-day proof and appropriate judgment supplied to you. Don't open antique wounds and go away the past wherein it's miles.

Speak For Yourself By Using "I"

It can be tempting to criticize the opportunity man or woman and placed terms in their mouth, but refrain from doing so. Try to speak best for yourself through the use of "I", together with "I'm feeling some resentment due to the fact…". "I" statements are un-blaming, all you are doing is communicating the manner you experience. This makes the opportunity man or woman experience less attacked which allows save you the state of affairs from escalating.

Deal With The Actual Argument

Arguments are frequently exacerbated via the reality that one issue isn't truly dealing with the opportunity aspect's function, however via a cool animated movie in their function. In terms of logical fallacies, this is called a Strawman. It refers to twisting someone's argument right right into a model that is less difficult to defeat, but have become now not what that character certainly said. Doing this isn't first-rate dishonest, however it guaranteed to provoke anger and a dismissive attitude from the alternative detail of the argument. Don't collect strawmen, cope with their real argument.

Give The Benefit Of The Doubt

When exchanges get heated there may be a bent to assume the worst in humans, probably that they may be being willfully ignorant or deceitful. Yet in popular maximum in reality humans bear in mind they'll be in the proper and performing consistent with their very personal enjoy of ethics; they may be not consciously searching for to undermine you. This isn't to say that there every now and then individuals who go through you sick-will, but it's miles right practice to start off by using way of assuming the great and giving the gain of the doubt. Allowing paranoia or insecurity to appear itself thru accusing human beings of sensible malice will close down the communication thru way of making your interlocutor antagonistic to your arguments. We need people to give us the advantage of the doubt and assume the nice, do your high-quality to reciprocate.

Be Polite

It is imperative to be well mannered at some point of the period of the argument. Don't yell, don't interrupt, keep eye contact mounted, thank them for taking note of you. Show them you have got were given admire for them as a way to elicit recognize yet again. If you lose their recognize you acquired't be able to convince them of some thing.

Be Confident

Being polite does no longer suggest being a pushover, however. Be confident in yourself and on your problem of view. Stand up straight, preserve eye contact, don't mumble. People are naturally inquisitive about self notion and in case you seem assured human beings will see you as greater persuasive.

Avoid Interrogations

Don't bombard your interlocutor with questions. Hitting someone with a fast-paced in no manner-ending litany of questions in the hopes of tripping them up, trapping them or complicated them is unhelpful and frequently insulting. Nobody enjoys feeling like their on trial or in an interrogation room, so have in mind of this at the identical time as asking questions.

"When thinking about the truth of a proposition, one is each engaged in an sincere appraisal of the evidence and logical arguments, or one isn't always."

-- Sam Harris

But Do Ask Questions

Asking questions can be enormously powerful in advancing the speak. The truth seeker Socrates evolved a way of thinking to research problems and display assumptions. Using the Socratic thinking approach gives as a minimum advantages. For one, it reveals to you the concept gadget of your conversational companion and second it gets your companion to look at their very own assumptions and beliefs. For instance: "How do assume she felt?" "How are you able to realise that's right?" "Why do expect that's the case?" Instead of telling humans what you agree with you studied or attempting to inform them the manner to count on, you could instead ask them to interact in self-reflection and permit them to schooling consultation if there are any issues with their detail of view.

Don't Be Belittling, Don't Put Down Their Ideas

If someone pushes an concept you discover silly or repellant, don't belittle them and don't condescend to them. Attempting to make others feel silly for having precise thoughts is a splendid way to steer them to enhance their defenses and reject what you've got were given to say. Even if it's far apparent to you why an concept is stupid, do not forget that it isn't apparent to them. Engage extensively with that idea and attempt to help them recognize why it isn't a extraordinary one.

Acknowledge How They Feel

If you have been angry or irritated with the aid of a few issue, wouldn't you want the other character to famend that? A easy acknowledgement of your accomplice's emotions can flow into an extended way in getting them to open up or de-escalating a controversy. Note that acknowledging someone's feelings is not just like agreeing with those feelings. If you enjoy the ones feelings are unjustified, you could give an explanation for that to the opposite man or woman however recognize that they're experiencing those feelings irrespective of what you reflect onconsideration on them.

Be Willing To Compromise

If you can't convince the possibility component of your angle, you can must compromise. If neither side is willing to offer an inch in a controversy, no solution will ever be reached. You can't bring your existence to a grinding halt and refuse to transport on till you get your manner. It is vital to be inclined to compromise, and to elicit that same willingness from your partner. Try to set less expensive phrases for the compromise you can each agree on. The terms don't want to be identical, but as a gesture of suitable faith they often are. What is maximum essential is that each of you could stay with the phrases, and that those phrases are adhered to.

Set Firm But Reasonable Boundaries

You want to set barriers in the argument and whilst trying to compromise. Don't permit a person convince you to perform a little factor this is morally wrong, or violates your autonomy truly because of the truth you are trying to compromise. That said, preserve your obstacles and desires less costly. Don't ask for big sacrifices from the opportunity person whilst sacrificing little yourself.

Do Your Research

If you need to influence someone you may want to have properly reasoned positions subsidized through using superb proof. You will also need to count on their responses and have rebuttals prepared for their arguments. This includes getting to know each aspects of your argument, every professionals and cons for your non-public principle or issue of view. The more you realize about the concern, the better off you're.

Present Them With The Facts

Once you have got were given completed the research present the ones records for your interlocutor in a way they may be able to understand. You want so that it will without a doubt state the facts, call the deliver, and offer an reason for why they may be relevant for your argument. You is probably an extended manner greater persuasive to others in case you come armed with relevant data instead of merely opinions. Remember also that your records want to come back from an remarkable, honest deliver and that you need a good way to provide an motive of why they again up your argument. You can't in reality throw records or information at a person, you want to assist them recognize how they manual your function.

Recognize When You've Hit A Wall

You must be capable of recognize at the same time as the communique has reached a standstill and neither thing is going to persuade the opportunity. If you have got have been given each provided your exceptional arguments and now appear to be protective the equal floor in a loop, it is time to prevent the talk. Upon accomplishing this problem, de-escalating if essential after which in a well mannered manner final the argument will allow each of you go to approximately your day and store each of you time.

Sleep On It

It's frequently stated that couples shouldn't visit mattress indignant, but sleep will permit you to get via an unpleasant argument. As you argue you get pressured out, greater emotional and much less eloquent. Giving each parties a threat to sleep on the subject will permit you each a threat to reevaluate simply precisely what is vital, and to return decrease back to the talk much less compelled/emotional.

Talk About It Over Food

Psychological research has proven that food makes humans greater amenable to receiving horrible news or having a tough discussion. Conversely, being hungry makes you more irritable and plenty much less rational. If you need to have a hard verbal exchange with someone, recollect doing it over dinner.

"Arguing with nameless strangers at the Internet is a sucker's mission because they almost always turn out to be—or to be indistinguishable from—self-righteous sixteen-12 months-olds proudly owning infinite portions of free time."

-- Neal Stephenson

Don't Build Weapon Stockpiles

When you're upset you may experience collectively with you need to sell off all of your grievances at one time, however this is counterproductive. Whipping out hassle after trouble can appear competitive, and bringing too many problems into the argument will excellent create confusion. It may even boom the chance of getting side-tracked with inappropriate subjects. Deal with one problem at a time to make development, normally the maximum urgent and relevant trouble.

Chapter 5: Overview Of The Word 'Argument'

1. What is an Argument?

An argument is a chain or collection of statements, propositions or justifications, which can be generally used to steer someone of a few component or to motive them to collect your thing of view, and finally, dragging them to in fact accept the belief thru your logical reasoning.

2. Why are Arguments given?

If you're a lion in an animal u . S . A ., and a few other lion attempts to go into your territory, you growl and roar to allow the possibility lion apprehend that this is your territory. He growls and roars again at you after finding out the water. Sometimes, the outsider stands down after a series of threats exchanged and the argument in the long run dissipates. Sometimes, a bloody fight begins if the possibility lion does not publish. Likewise, you argue collectively together with your parents, siblings, or buddies, enforcing your element of view on them and proving your self right. There is lots of distinction among an difficulty and a quarrel. The motive of an problem is to area your factor of view in the front of others, instead of to impress your target marketplace or to assault your opponent. The number one intention of an problem is to make different human beings be given as actual with correct in what you tell them through providing them right motives in help of your opinion or end. Such reasons can be common with the useful useful resource of the opponent sports. Argument isn't always the denial of what the opposite character says. Sometimes, the opposite individual says something wrong and you understand that he is at fault, however you need to provide arguments to clear up your dispute. You need to offer him a few logics or motives maturely that depict him to be incorrect and compel him to absolutely receive what you're pronouncing.

three. Stages of an Argument

There are 3 one-of-a-type tiers or steps of an hassle. These encompass Premises, Inference and Conclusion.

a. Premises of an Argument

A premise is essentially a statement that induces or justifies a prevent, claimed through manner of an argument. More exactly, it is an assumption that some detail is actual. Premises of an problem are one or more propositions which is probably obligatory to maintain an argument and that they should be explicitly stated. They are the motives, evidences or proofs for accepting the argument, and moreover, its end. Premises are indicated with the aid of fantastic phrases, collectively with "manifestly", "due to the truth", "thinking about the fact that" and so forth. When you fall in an trouble, you offer a declaration. In order to justify your declaration, you need to make grounds and take nice theses without any consideration. These are in fact the premises of your argument. So, if your opponent accepts those premises, you truely deliver him to virtually take delivery of your cease of the argument. In common sense, declarative sentences, referred to as premises, combined with some exclusive declarative sentence, known as quit, are required with the aid of a controversy in phrases of not unusual experience. Now, to make clear the idea of premises, I will display you a sample argument.

1. Going to fitness center every day for exercising continues your frame in shape.

2. Oliver has sound health and his body is in shape.

3. Oliver is going every day to the gym for exercising.

Here, statements 1 and 2 are premises, even as announcement 3 is a give up.

b. Inference of an Argument

Further propositions are received by the use of the use of the premises of the argument. This system is referred to as inference. We start with one or extra propositions, that have been enormous in inference, essential us to derive a modern-day proposition. Several types of legitimate inference are also mentioned. Some inferences are used to similarly derive new inferences. Inferences are indicted via certain terms, together with "therefore", "therefore" or "manner that".

c. Conclusion of an Argument

We ultimately arrive at every different proposition, the belief of the argument. The give up of the argument is commonly stated because the very last and the very last degree of inference. It is affirmed and derived on the idea of the premises and the inference. Conclusions are indicated with the resource of a few precise phrases. When you glide in the direction of greater complex arguments, the ones be a part of positive premises to a unmarried stop or a number of conclusions may be drawn from the premises, which then act as premises for further conclusions.

Chapter 6: Constructing A Logical Argument

1. What is Logic?

Logic is the technology of proof, reasoning, inference or thinking. Logic essentially lets in us to analyze a bit of reasoning whether or not or now not it's far accurate or no longer. We test out the reasoning to be legitimate or invalid. You do now not absolutely want to take a look at nicely judgment for reasoning successfully. However, while you gather or analyze an argument, a chunk easy information of proper judgment is useful. You have to realize the manner to apply common experience and whether or not or now not the best judgment is the right tool for the activity.

2. Basic Concepts

Propositions, furthermore called statements, are the constructing blocks of a logical argument. A proposition is certainly a announcement that may either be wrong or accurate. For instance;

- London is the capital of England.

- Average human existence span is 60 years.

- Dogs are colorblind.

The above statements may be subjects of arguments on the concept in their nature of being right or fake.

3. Types of Arguments

Arguments are labeled into traditional sorts, deductive and inductive.

a. Deductive Argument

The conclusive evidence of its conclusions is provided by using the use of manner of a deductive argument. In this form of argument, it's miles real that if the premises are actual, give up want to be actual. A deductive argument can each be legitimate or invalid. Deductive arguments are regularly taken into consideration as most convincing and rigorous.

b. Inductive Argument

If the premises provide some proof that the conclusion is real, then it's miles an inductive argument. Inductive arguments can not be legitimate or invalid. Instead, they're higher or worse than one-of-a-kind arguments.

Chapter 7: Why Do We Feel The Need Of An Arguement?

Let's bear in mind a situation. You have become first-rate friends with a person previously, but now, you preserve on preventing all the time. You are caused through the minor subjects said through your accomplice. You feel degraded, devalued and attacked, and as a result, you react spontaneously. As precise humans react in certainly one of a type techniques, so might likely you yell or walk out of the door, or slam the door near or refuse to talk to all people. When u appearance decrease lower back, it is probably difficult for you to inform the way you even have been given into the argument in the first region. There might be a few component very diffused from the opportunity individual that grew to turn out to be you angry, like rolled eyes, a smirk, terrible tone of voice or a certain frame posture. This subtly of your companion brought approximately you to react likewise or harshly, and your response might be to be the same and specific thing that drives your accomplice crazy. He is mad on you whether you are saying hurtful things in any other case you depart your companion feeling deserted fleeing the battlefield. This is a vicious cycle.

1. Responses of Brain

Although we want near relationships with every unique, we're despite the fact that hard-confused out for survival. It is natural that whilst you sense threatened, you lodge to reflex-like reactions, like combat, flight and freeze, to guard your self from being harm extra. Your thoughts tries to investigate the in all likelihood final consequences of a quarrel and judges if there may be enough power to combat and win or enough time to get away. You anticipate to your self whether or no longer staying quiet is the quality approach if you need to live on. These responses are not opted rationally. Instead, they are brought about via a few external stimuli, causing your brain to proper away fireside. Such a response is compulsory to live on bodily or emotionally, because of the fact the mind has been created in methods to optimize and technique those self-safety responses. The problem is that even as you're discussing an uncomfortable issue along side your companion or falling in a excessive argument, your response is probably exaggerated. Sometimes, you start an problem and from time to time, argument is your response. When you fall in an problem, your mind receives a sign of a few element horrific which you do now not seem to like, it's far ignited up and sends again a signal which will respond spontaneously. You can control the responses of your mind within the course of an issue. It takes a whole lot of exercising, time and expert sport to train new techniques of responding in your thoughts. This manner, you may settle arguments or probable win them.

2. Constructive Arguments

If you argue for extra than five minutes with someone, then maximum likely, it's miles about you, no longer about them or their actions. You have to discover a deeper truth in this announcement every time you get indulged in an trouble. You must understand what is going on inner your thoughts. For that, take a deep breathe, test in with yourself and study thoroughly your thoughts. If you're ignorant of your kingdom of thoughts, you can't argue correctly. You want to discover ways to get keep of while you confront those feelings and thoughts. If you are agonized, allow your self to feel that struggling. But, do no longer allow that pain have an effect on your actions. Take steps towards solving your issues in desire to giving upward thrust to greater troubles. So, whenever we argue with a person, it's miles the depiction of our internal feelings. If we realize this hassle with a groovy mind, then argument may be an immensely exquisite a part of love and lifestyles. If you want to be in an extended-time period relationship, like familial, romantic or platonic, it is compulsory to discover ways to argue constructively.

Chapter 8: Why Your Arguments Fail?

Arguments are a ought to as a way to warn, assist, love, lead, examine, create and in the long run, to revel in justice. The artwork of argument is same to the artwork of dwelling. You argue due to the truth you want to and also due to the fact existence itself desires it. You often fail to win an problem. This is due to the truth there are positive strategies to argue. When you do not understand the right manner to argue, you can't win any argument. Winning an trouble is a potential. Some are born with this expertise, having outstanding convincing strength, and so, they're capable of with out problem win arguments. Some want to test this abilities.

Reasons of Failure of your Arguments

Below are stated some reasons why your arguments fail. Once you understand the motives of your failure, you can art work upon them, and ultimately, win all sorts of arguments.

1. Fear of Losing

You won't need to argue. In fact, you do no longer enjoy appropriate about the individuals who argue. So, when someone argues with you, you try to get alongside. You attempt your notable to avoid arguments due to the fact you observed, you may lose if you may argue. This worry of losing turns into a deliver of your failure.

2. Silence is considered the Best Option

You might in all likelihood assume that arguments just motive hassle. It is difficult as a way to argue with humans you want. It can also moreover moreover get your buddy or fellow indignant, and alienate your family. You are afraid to argue and also you bear in thoughts silence the satisfactory option to select in this sort of scenario. This state of affairs leaves you in a non arguing country all the time, even if your opponents argues with you. Ultimately, you continuously revel in a failed argument.

three. Lack of the Talent to Argue

Winning an problem is a skillful act. There are top notch techniques you want to apprehend to win an argument. You may additionally suppose that only top notch audio system and orators win arguments maximum of the time and also you yourself do now not very personal the recognize-a way to win arguments constantly. This skills isn't always inborn, you need to achieve this abilties.

four. Focus on Winning

When you argue, simply don't focus on prevailing all the time. You have to influence the other man or woman civilly. Arguing is not nice about winning, it's far approximately conveying your component of view to the opportunity character and convince him logically to certainly acquire it. If you interest on triumphing the argument, it might lead you to fail the argument.

five. Doubting your Powers

You won't don't forget your self a powerful individual. You is probably afraid that the opportunity person is lots greater effective than you. You doubt that in place of convincing your fighters, you can get convinced via them thru their incredible powers to argue. Doubting your powers to argue effectively drags you to failure.

6. Not revealing all Truths

If you lie approximately some element or do not screen the entire reality in the course of a controversy and get stuck, the other person will in no manner take delivery of as authentic with you yet again. In this way, you lose now not most effective arguments, but your integrity as well.

7. Illogical Arguments

An argument need to own logics and reasoning. Illogical arguments are in no way processed and are destined to fail in the end. If you argue without giving affordable logics, the alternative person will in no way be satisfied. Your statement can be taken into consideration illogical and will now not take transport of any concept, crucial your argument to extraordinary failure.

8. Use of Wrong Words

If you do no longer choose out out accurate phrases in an issue, you're maximum probably to fail. Selection of terms for a controversy rely variety masses. If you use harsh phrases, you are in all likelihood to harm others causing your failure. Likewise, emotionless talks can't create a persuading impact on others.

9. Weak Structure of an Argument

If you do now not make grounds for your argument, it'll not create a first rate impact for your opponent. If you do not resource your argument via justifications and logics, its content material fabric fabric and shape live inclined, and you'll be no longer going to win the argument.

10. Confused Arguments

If you aren't clean approximately what you actually need, in case you are having confusions on your mind, you're definitely going to give puzzled statements. Naturally, at the same time as you do now not recognize your self, then how can you count on others to recognize you? Confusion is the primary supply of failure of your arguments.

11. Use of Sarcasm, Scorn and Ridicule

It is taken into consideration a very impolite motion in case your argument possesses sarcasm, scorn and ridicule. The one-of-a-type man or woman may also moreover get irritated or damage. This way, he/she will in no manner pay attention to you. Use of Sarcasm, ridicule and scorn will purpose the failure of your argument.

12. Depiction of Arrogance or Insolence

If your attitude and conduct while arguing are an define of conceitedness or insolence, then the alternative character will in no way pay attention to you. You weaken and come to be worse your argument via smug and insolent conduct.

13. Losing your Temper

When you argue, you want to be affected person. If you lose your mood and are ignited up at the equal time as arguing, you start yelling and shouting. It will become extra like a fight than a problem, therefore, failing you badly.

14. Not Listening to Your Opponent

If you do not listen for your opponent, in case you do not go through in thoughts his factor of view, he/she by no means prefers to pay attention to you. Even if he/she listens to you, they will now not respect your trouble of view. This reasons your argument to fail.

15. Igniting up Your Opponent

If you ignite up your opponent and deliver upward thrust to his rage and fury thru your words or via using private assaults within the path of an issue, this spills water over all of your efforts of winning an issue. Such movement leads you to mere failure.

16. Pessimistic Approach

If you fall into an trouble with a pessimistic technique then you may not have the capability to persuade the other individual and you can fail the argument. Negative thinking does now not anything however drag you into the dungeons of failure.

17. Diverting the Topic

During a hassle, if you do no longer maintain on with the actual difficulty rely, you're probably to lose the argument. Changing the issue or diverting from the real assignment depend range weakens your argument and the alternative individual will lose their hobby in what you assert. Therefore, they may now not be satisfied by using the use of your arguments ultimately causing you to fail.

Chapter 9: How To Win Any Argument

Arguments are one of the most hard emotional situations in existence. Conflict offers rise to blood stress and anxiety, whether or not or now not or now not it's miles with someone you despise or love or do not even realise. Some people do their great to avoid arguments while others generally seem prepared to fall into them. If you fall in among those extremes, then you definitely won't choose to argue, but you're prepared to acquire this on the same time as wanted. In this case, the question concerning you is a way to make the argument pass your manner.

1. Ultimate Strategies for Getting Your Point Across

A lot of studies has been finished on struggle and battle choice. Conflicts can be resolved among couples in near relationships, which in the end enhance their capability to live collectively. You can be immensely benefited through way of preserving your tongue on the proper time. You do no longer want to fall in useless arguments and debates, which do not anything except waste some time and get worse your relationships. In a problem, you experience specific varieties of emotions, which can be precipitated via some matters. These embody your perception which you need to be right, your appraisal that you are dropping, to what amount you like the possibility person, desire to obtain the honor of the onlookers and the impact of the alternative individual's reactions. Sometimes, a problem ends resulting in yelling, the warring parties flying insults over every unique and the conclusion no longer being drawn. So, you must have a have a look at the proper procedures to deal with the argument to keep away from it from converting right into a conflict. Once you lose your temper and get indignant, you're much less probable to win. This is because of the fact you lose the capacity of repute your logical grounds. Arguments are not obtained with the beneficial useful resource of the right human beings, however through the human beings armed with proper abilties and techniques. Such humans can effects flip tables on others.

2. Magical Tips and Tricks of Winning Any Argument and Getting What You Want

Keeping all of the above problems in thoughts, I will introduce you to positive argument-triumphing system. Below are said a few magical suggestions and pointers of winning any argument, an great manner to assist you to your destiny debates. If you follow all of pointers, you'll be popularity at a very sturdy vicinity on your destiny arguments.

a. Get Rid of the Fear of Losing

Fear is your nice pal and foe. If you do no longer argue due to the fact you are frightened of losing, you then definately need to remove your worry. You ought to revel in the courage to create the argument so that it will verify your self. You want to boom a self belief in yourself that you may do it, you may argue correctly. Just kick out this obstacle of fear in your way to fulfillment.

b. Know the Complete Facts

Sometimes, it takes region which you continuously argue about something, and afterwards, you come back face to face with the truth that you had been absolutely incorrect. But, you still stay with your weapons because of the truth you do now not want to lose besides. This isn't always a absolutely high-quality manner of winning an trouble. Just ponder over each the sides of a story earlier than you're making any bloopers your self. This manner, you may in no way lose whether or not or not the problem is a truely vital career, a trivia or a courting assignment. Do now not u . S . That a few issue is sincerely actual, lest you are absolutely certain of it. Debating a topic with someone who's virtually growing his arguments at the fly, is especially traumatic. So, do not do it to others. It is appreciated in case you take pleasure in such arguments that can be acquired with the useful aid of you, based totally totally on records.

c. Look into the alternative individual's Perspective

Looking into the opportunity person's angle does now not mean which you want to trust her or him. You must be capable of see the place out of your opponent's eyes, so one can win an problem. When you step in the thoughts of your opponent, you could take a look at out what's influencing him. He might be feeling stressful, threatened or angry. He may realize a few element which you do not seem to recognize. The temperature of the argument is decreased via showing empathy, allowing every of you to return returned to a give up and a resolution.

d. Listen for your Opponent and be Open-minded

One of the worst techniques of winning a controversy is to end up shielding. If your opponent senses which you aren't willing to bear in mind any alternatives and you are cussed on your position, then he'll undertake a bad impact of you. If you be aware of your opponent and deliver his function a considerate evaluation, then your proposed solution appears far extra practical. This will drag your opponent to your side without doing each extraordinary problem than listening. You allow the scenario to definitely remedy itself with the resource of giving your opponent a chance to talk.

e. Control your Emotions

Emotions play a tremendous feature throughout arguments through manner of changing your manner of appraising the scenario. It may be very critical to adjust your emotions. If you lose your mood, it'll damage your capability to assume wisely, as well as, giving upward thrust for your opponent's wrath and anger. Opposing the alternative individual bitterly is not the right shape of hassle to do. It in no manner is your precedence. Losing temper worsens the argument and enhance the fight upwards. If you emerge as calm within the midst of any argument, do not count on that you can seem inclined. Instead, this can be an outline that you could exercise power of will and can earn you elements. Controlling your emotions within the direction of an problem extinguishes the fireplace of hatred and bitterness. Once every of you emerge as more cheap and take a more reasoned mind-set, the argument may additionally moreover loosen up proper there.

f. Move inside the route of resolving the Argument

The phrase 'argument' hides in it awful emotions and bitterness. In the midst of a problem, it's miles hard on the manner to visualise your self accepting the other man or woman's aspect of view with your self-understand and dignity intact. You can assume extra absolutely with the aid of the use of invoking the feeling of choice that the argument may be resolved, due to the fact you offer you with modern answers to the arguments in case you stay hopeful. Once you flow into in the direction of the answer, it's going to enhance your probabilities of prevailing the argument through manner of sheer pressure of proper judgment. Once you take delivery of as true with that there can be a way out, you might discover a way out of the locked battle of wills. Such a second in a controversy leads you right now to victory.

g. Respect Your Opponent

Sometimes, at the same time as you argue together with your near ones, you might get what you want, however it worsens your dating. A a achievement argument stays compartmentalized within a courting. Don't permit the argument spoil the policies of your relationship. Don't insult, degrade or humiliate your opponent in the course of an difficulty. Don't get private during the dispute and do no longer say harsh matters about the other man or woman. Never hotel to name calling. If you start criticizing your opponent, it's far apparent which you are playing dirty to defend your view. Such insults cause dropping an problem. It is compulsory to recognize your opponent in case you want to win the argument.

h. Be Silent

Once you have got made a sturdy argument, be silent and allow your opponent talk. Let him oppose you in his quality feasible way. He will fumble and bluster, arming you with new guns to assault him. This will in the end lead him to stroll faraway from the communicate, which leaves you due to the fact the winner of the argument. Most of the arguments are gained via now not arguing at all. Make your request for your opponent and even as he turns down your request, continue to be silent. As no character likes silence, so your silence may also need to render your opponent annoying and worrying. He need to in the end supply in to interrupt your silence and to get out of this uncomfortable situation.

i. Ask Questions

When your opponent gives an issue and states a reality, plunge into the depth of what he said. After analyzing the reality thoroughly, provide you with such questions which is probably capable of revealing the failings of that argument. These are the questions like "Can you u . S . A . Any example of this?" or "Knowing all the data, wouldn't it now not appear practical?"

These questions are amongst those that could trick your opponent brilliantly in telling the fact and he is going to concede if he's honest or leave the communication in anger otherwise. So, in the long run, you may win the argument.

j. Stick to the Actual Argument

When the opposite man or woman falls prone in an difficulty, he's going to try to divert the challenge. He will try and get you entangled in a whole new argument without being placed via manner of you. This is a lure, don't fall for it. You should be capable of returning to the unique scenario take into account proper now. Avoid lingering onto notable topics in case you but have one unfinished subject count number accessible.

correct enough. Fundamentals to be Defined

There are some critical truths which want to be agreed upon via each the arguing parties. To make it smooth, take an instance, you argue along with your opponent that God has written Bible, but if he does no longer accept as true with in God, then there can be no point of arguing. You should debate the existence of God first. So, without a doubt start with the essential factors, offer arguments and counter-arguments, and flow into on as quick as every component is showed through way of not unusual experience.

l. Don't Attack

Telling your opponent blatantly that he is incorrect, isn't always an awesome idea.

Instead, you should depict via appropriate arguments that he is inaccurate. Your opponent may also get angry at this. You must be humble in the argument and depict right will. It lifts your image in the the front of your opponent.

m. Get Your Opponent on Your Side

If you're making such statements approximately that you already apprehend that your opponent has the same opinion with them, then you could get your opponent by way of manner of way of your issue. This places you in a completely robust vicinity inside the argument. If you get your opponent by the usage of your issue thru effective techniques, then you can have received a intellectual battle. He considers you not his opponent, however a comrade. This is a completely effective approach in winning a trouble.

n. Soft and Steady Tone

You need to in no way growth your voice while you're arguing. You want to live peaceful and calm all of the time. If you speak louder, so does your opponent, and the stop surrender quit result is a shouting healthful. Avoid violent acts and communicate politely as this makes you seem wiser and your opponent listens to you. The character with the loudest voice isn't the winner of the argument, but the man or woman with the most compelling arguments is of course. So, preserve your tone clean and regular.

o. The Power of Words

The fulfillment of your argument is based upon upon the content cloth and form of your debate. Selection of the proper and convincing terms plays a exquisite position on this regard. You can't underestimate the strength of terms. Strong and convincing terms compose a powerful argument, increasing your opportunities of prevailing in the long run.

Chapter 10: The Biggest Enemy To Decisions

Have you ever observed yourself trying to make a choice about your life, and yet you in no way look like able to make a selection? What is it that appears to be protecting you again? I anticipate that inertia is the most important enemy for alternatives. This inertia can show up in severa approaches, like locating the exquisite time, now not being "smart enough," nearly there, the recognition quo, if handiest, and in loads of other approaches. These subjects are excuses and lies that too many humans tell themselves each day. What if there has been a manner to triumph over this hassle and bypass in advance to your desire-making gadget?

This may additionally want to sound too correct to be actual, however it may be. A massive thing within the choice-making approach is worry. Fear is the primary motive for inertia in making choices. However, I want you to recall the acronym for FEAR: False, Evidence, Appearing, Real.

When you end up involved or disturbing, your thoughts can with out problem start racing one hundred miles a minute, and it will become tough to shut it off. Your thoughts ultimately ends up racing closer to those imaginary cliffs in your thoughts. Ninety% of the time, even though, all of these fears you experience never show up, so there has been pretty a few emotional electricity wasted.

Fear moreover has the strength to kill your desire to fulfill your desires. We all typically typically tend to have a bias that makes us worry loss greater so than we need achievement. If you spend all your time targeted on fear, you acquired't acquire success. The wonderful difficulty to do in that case is to voice your fears and face them. You can update the ones fears together with your prolonged-time period desires. You can then use the desires you have got were given as your compass for your thoughts sports activities and concept techniques. This will permit you to feel extra positivity as opposed to to fill your mind with horrible fears that hold you from making picks.

Living reactively to subjects isn't going to help you meet your inner most wishes. If you live your lifestyles with the aid of speeding from one issue to the subsequent after which come to recognize you haven't in fact done something, is that any better than residing in inertia. When it involves an trouble, being reactive is the nice way to get a person to prevent listening. At that point, you're using most effective your feelings and now not your brain.

All of this can result in dissonance with what you're doing and your values in life.

A brilliant way to art work through this is thru the usage of clean questions. When it includes you decide, attempt asking, "What makes this well well worth my time?", "What is inflicting me to revel in stuck?", "How does this fit up with who I am?" and whilst you look lower back at the subjects you have have been given accomplished, seeking to decide out what recommendation you'll deliver your self, know-how what you recognize now.

Getting caught in the choice-making technique also may be as a result of you make a decision via one frame of reference or the usage of one method. Has this ever occurred to you? You make a preference approximately a particular route you want to absorb lifestyles, however it doesn't seem the way you desired it to, so you don't try anymore. That's no longer useful, so the following time you find out yourself in that function, try to ask yourself the ones questions:

1. Rationale – "What are the professionals and cons of going after both preference?"

2. Relational – "How is this route of movement going to have an effect on those round me?"

three. Alignment – "How well does this suit up with my passions, values, and calling?"

four. Spiritual – "What choice goes to great align with my faith?"

5. Cost – "What is this going to rate me in terms of time and belongings? What wouldn't it rate if I don't do this?"

6. Risk/Reward – "What is the payoff for each possibility? What is the possibility fee of every? What are the risks, and the way should they be minimized?"

Motive-Driven Actions

When you pick out among matters, A and B, you every decide upon one over the possibility, or you are indifferent to either preference. This concept doesn't expect any shape of manner involved in making the selection. Therefore, preference between A or B should live the identical irrespective of whether or not or no longer or now not A or B is the recognition-quo alternative. That technique if making a decision upon A to B, you then definately definitely ought to pick out A irrespective of what.

However, the repute quo is a big player in the approach in terms of preference-making and inertia. This will become a bigger trouble for you who are detached to A or B. When you are apathetic, you'll probable go along with the recognition-quo alternative. You received't act to alternate the popularity quo except you have were given been pushed to reap this thru a few form of motivation. With the intellectual law of inertia, humans will frequently want to hold the popularity quo till they will be driven to trade it with the resource of a few type of intellectual motivation.

A character dreams some form of intellectual stress, the motive to get them to determine that works for them and not simplest for the repute quo. While I made a factor of announcing that a person detached to their selections has a tendency to go with the popularity-quo choice, irrespective of the truth that they skip in the direction of their values, they also can be hit with the aid of inertia due to the reality the options are fuzzy ill-described.

For example, Kivetz and Simonson (2002) placed that humans will use the relative strive of others as a reference to judging in reality the amount of strive that goes with the Reward. Specifically, within the event that they have been demonstrated a "deal" that changed into particularly better for a incredible character than for the common man or woman, it modified into plenty extra attractive, masses just so it is probably favored over the more popular alternative. Their test supplied diners a rewards software where they may get a unfastened meal after they paid for a certain extensive style of food. They positioned the sushi fanatics preferred a praise software software that required them to shop for 10 sandwiches and 10 sushi platters to one that best required them to buy 10 sandwiches. The sushi fanatics noticed an advantage to that possibility because of the reality they may have possibly eaten the sushi except. With this relative gain, the sushi lovers felt they had been getting a "good buy" in an absolute feel.

A smooth rationalization of that is that the thoughts is constantly searching out for the suitable alternative. It doesn't suggest the man or woman is lazy, but the thoughts doesn't like having to do a number of paintings. If because of this sticking with the popularity quo, then the character will preserve on with it until he can convince himself otherwise.

In almost each preference you're making, there can be a degree of worry of the diagnosed and unknown. We can also want to have alternatives that don't have uncomplicated benefits, but we though need to make a choice. To overcome that inertia, you want to consciously art work via the choice-making technique with questions and probable outside help. You need to discover your values and the motivations that force you. Later on, we are capable of be going over the way to figure out what you stand for, that would help with the choice-making method.

The unknown can only become diagnosed if you take the time to find out it.

Chapter 11: Keep Your Options Open

How often do you find out your self suffering to make your mind up approximately some factor?

Everybody makes severa alternatives each day. Some might be pretty easy, like figuring out to get off the bed, what to consume, what to position on, which emails to answer to, however there are exceptional selections that are masses greater complex that make you have got a study all of your options like creating a career trade or identifying in case you need to move. You'll ought to begin searching at some necessities, collectively with having to move returned to highschool. If you want to transport, you want to begin searching at your charge variety and identifying what form of housing alternatives are open to you.

When you face the ones options, you may actually study one desire or test all of them at one time. If you are trying to determine which software you would really like to interview, hiring managers would possibly probable test one character's resume at a time, create an opinion approximately them, and float directly to the subsequent one. You can also unfold out all of the resumes on their table, test and evaluate them, after which determine who you would like to interview. An investor must take a look at the data of 1 in each in their mutual budget at one time, or you may look at them at one time on a spreadsheet.

In one study published in "Organizational Behavior and Human Decision Processes," they looked at how searching at your alternatives should have an effect on a person's desire. They asked for volunteers within the United States on an internet panel. They did seven particular experiments, and the volunteers were asked to choose out from the options that had been each proven or one after the other. Some of their picks had been fairly clean, like which coloration shirt to buy; extra complicated selections like which charity you want to help proper now. Most of the time, they located that human beings need to choose out the tremendous possibility after they checked out all their alternatives at the equal time in choice to looking at them in my opinion (Basu & Savani, 2017).

The first time round, they requested 201 online volunteers to choose a unique model of five kinds of electronics like microwaves, laptops, televisions, and so on. For each product, there had been six one in every of a kind models to pick out out from; every of them had distinct attributes. For each laptop, the volunteers have been given statistics about the charge of the processor, battery existence, assure, storage capability, and RAM. Their excellent opportunity can be the version with the maximum vital charge for every function (Basu & Savani, 2017).

They randomly decided on half of of of the volunteers to check the options together. For each considered one of the goods, they checked out the information of each model at one time on a computer after which picked one. The extraordinary volunteers have been asked to look at the alternatives in my view. All the facts approximately one model is probably confirmed on one display, the following version on a completely unique display display, and so on. After they'd looked at all of the models for a specific product, they will pass a number of the displays to pick the first-rate one. They decided the volunteers who checked out all of the options one at a time picked the splendid opportunity approximately seventy five% of the time. The people who looked at the alternatives all at the identical time picked the high-quality product, about eighty 4% (Basu & Savani, 2017).

Within the equal take a look at, they accrued a few unique 500 volunteers who were requested to visualize proudly owning a eating place. They had to order their weekly materials for a few gadgets like ketchup, milk, and many others. They needed to select out one in all five numerous carriers; each company had quoted a high-quality charge for the products. The volunteers ought to determine to buy milk from one provider which have come to be selling a case of 35 gallons for $seventy 3.50. In assessment, a one-of-a-kind one modified into asking $69.90 for 29 gallons, and many others. The options have been designed in order that there ought to constantly be one supplier who had each unit at the lowest fee, however the volunteers needed to do a little math to parent out which one turned into the bottom charge. Just just like the alternative experiments, that they had half of the volunteers take a look at the vendors together to make their choice, on the equal time because the opportunity 1/2 looked at the providers for my part. The volunteers who checked out the options in my view decided the most inexpensive agency approximately fifty 5 % of the time, but the volunteers who looked at all of the records together determined the cheapest approximately sixty one % of the time. This same pattern have come to be decided in other experiments, too, when they managed the volunteers' math ability (Basu & Savani, 2017).

Why can we make higher selections while we are capable to check all our alternatives at one time in place of in my opinion?

One viable cause is when all the facts is inside the the the front human beings, we are able to have a take a look at all our options better and discover the quality alternatives a whole lot less complex. Suppose we ought to study a number of options in my view. In that case, we need to shape a judgment approximately every character one and then appearance decrease lower back and compare them time and again another time.

These opportunities had been examined in first rate experiments that used comparable setups. Still, they requested the volunteers to put in writing down any mind that that that they'd had at the equal time as making their picks. They used software known as LIWC that places terms into various lessons to take a look at the responses they wrote down.

Again, the results had been the equal in that when alternatives had been studied in my opinion; they didn't make as clever of a preference. The volunteers who looked at all their options at one time used terms and phrases that cautioned they were deeper in concept, which consist of "I expect that B is extra than A" or "Hence, I experience that A is the best choice." These findings useful aid the idea that human beings evaluate their options masses more thoroughly at the equal time as they can see them at one time.

We haven't been recognized to generally examine our alternatives at the same time. In some distinctive have a have a look at, hundred volunteers had been requested to go through in mind some choices they'd made within the past and were asked whether or no longer they normally looked at their alternatives in my view or together. These volunteers stated that they'll take a look at their alternatives in my view for spherical half in their alternatives.

At the identical time, groups don't help human beings see all their alternatives at one time. When looking at net sites of the top lifestyles insurance corporations and vehicle producers, they positioned that every internet net website had precise pages for all their products that permit clients reflect onconsideration on every product in my view. Still, some internet net sites allow human beings to have a look at various merchandise all together on one display display screen. Many websites did have a assessment tool, but it simplest lets people compare some alternatives.

The manner we examine and gift our alternatives also can moreover seem like trivial topics. Research has shown that it may majorly effect our picks.

Decisions Are Harder to Make When You Have a Lot of Options

When you're confronted with a lot of alternatives, you decide is lots harder. In some new studies, they use fictional dating profiles and cardiovascular measures to locate answers. Despite all the opportunities that having many alternatives deliver us, wanting to really pick out one will create what's referred to as a "paralyzing paradox."

We want to have alternatives, but even as we want to actually face figuring out among all the alternatives, the whole element takes a flip for the more excessive.

We need to make the proper choices, however there are times on the same time as we don't sense like we are able to. The mixture of considering the low capability and excessive stakes might also make a contribution to our deep-seated fears that we are able to make the wrong desire. This can kill our desire-making approach.

To help you control what seems unmanageable, you want to reflect onconsideration on all the relative significance of all of the options in front of you. Deciding what you consume or what you watch doesn't define who you are. It may be useful if you have to determine to have a few suggestions in mind approximately what you want out of the preferred preference. Doing this will now not help you lessen the range of selections, but disposing of some alternatives that don't trust your suggestions can raise confidence so that you can accept as true with your intuition to make the right choice.

Studies have set up that having to make selections has been related to terrible effects. Still, this have a look at great looked at factors about making choices: how a person thinks about their capability to make top alternatives and how precious their selection is.

Having alternatives is an appealing situation that does communicate about autonomy and freedom. All the developing on line amusement and buying may be overwhelming. Just looking for a contemporary-day jacket on line can come up with hundreds of alternatives. One online provider furnished more than 7,000 options. Online dating may additionally additionally want to have lots and hundreds of subscribers enrolled.

Having selections does look like a high-quality concept till you want to make that choice. You love to have choices, however at the equal time as you're confronted with choosing from endless alternatives, the whole technique hits a useless forestall.

Research has proven that most humans will regret their alternatives. Still, the researchers suggest that this paradox of liking to have selections after which getting indignant via using those alternatives takes place immediately. It is a totally charming transition.

For this have a examine, they asked for 500 volunteers for 3 severa studies, of those used psychophysiological measures. They had their volunteers observe thru some relationship profiles and asked them to pick out out their outstanding associate. Since they had been used to psychophysiological measures, they favored the volunteers to stand a choice that demanded a few interest and engaged them (Saltsman et al., 2019).

The way they measured the volunteers protected the volunteer's coronary heart expenses. When they care about a desire, their coronary coronary heart fee will boom beat tougher. They additionally checked out one-of-a-kind measures, which incorporates how a terrific deal blood the coronary heart pumped and what type of the blood vessels dilated, which showed the volunteer's degree of self perception.

These outcomes display that when we are faced with a big type of selections to decide from in region of a smaller amount, volunteers' blood vessels and hearts showed that they determined their alternatives to be more overwhelming and more vital. This befell whilst they have been considering about their selections.

Even despite the truth that greater studies are wanted, this can assist us recognize the relationship amongst awful outcomes and choice overload. Looking at someone's evaluations also can assist us comprehend greater about the negative desire overload and approaches to save you them.

"Choices are the hinges of destiny." - Edwin Markham

Chapter 12: No Decision Is Still A Decision

People who've no longer on time you make a decision will come to find out that they've decided, and there's a risk that it wasn't in their first rate interest. William James, an American psychologist, and fact seeker stated, "No preference is, in itself, a selection." And there are few superb sayings that have as masses which means that regarding selection-making.

More often than not, humans will revel in inertia and hide this incapacity to transport with excuses. We've all said such things as:

- "We're watching for topics to alternate."

- "We're no longer at the identical web web page but."

- "I'm too busy to think about it proper now."

And all of these exceptional rationalizations that human beings can offer you with.

However, in actual existence, you will be you make a decision without identifying it. It can be the selection to hold the recognition quo. That is a beautifully valid preference, so long as you are good enough with it.

The problem with this kind of approach to choice-making is that it is going to give some thing or someone else manipulate rather than being proactive. However, there can be instances in life at the same time as permitting matters to spread the manner they want to can work flawlessly for you and come up with the first-class final outcomes. For example, you can spend years stressful about if you need to make a circulate out of your organization. During that point, some coverage modifications take region that certainly impact you, which magically restoration the situation (Diamond, 2019).

Unfortunately, there also are times at the same time as you do nothing except desire that matters will alternate, and don't exercise session that manner. There may be times to your lifestyles whilst topics trade for the better and location you in a better role than you've got been in advance than, however it can moreover region you in a worse characteristic.

Let me positioned this in attitude for you. Let's say that an guide, we'll call him Sam, has been running at his interest for 15 years. He has mentioned, on numerous sports activities, that his enterprise isn't serving him nicely. He doesn't see any room for boom for him and that his task is limiting what he can achieve. He is aware of that there are special companies that would work better for him (Diamond, 2019).

Sam is aware about all of these things, however he appears to be genuinely uncomfortable. He makes decent cash, maintains all of his clients, and has the time to train his daughter's softball business enterprise.

Still, he has had this nagging feeling that there can be extra he desires. He has even met with one of a kind agencies to speak approximately his options. Now, it's proper all the way down to him making a decision. He has the choice of leaving or staying, yet he can't seem to make that choice.

Why?

It is probably that he hasn't determined an opportunity that is better than what he currently has. He hasn't become sad enough. He is caught.

Either way, even as he can also appear like he hasn't determined, he has. He has selected to stay in which he is for some thing reason. Now, matters may additionally want to play out for him well. The problems he has along along with his present day technique are labored out, and it will become his outstanding undertaking. However, things should worsen, and he need to find out him worse off than he changed into.

While no longer you decide stays a desire, it may now not be a clever preference. Just like with some different alternatives you are making, you have to take a look at the larger picture. Figure out in case your preference of no longer selecting is out of fear or due to the reality you absolutely be given as authentic with matters will training consultation. The truth of the state of affairs may be that you are glad sufficient in that you're. If so, then deciding on not to decide is a top notch decision to make.

But don't try to idiot yourself. Dig deep, and figure out if it is able to be that you are genuinely fearful of asking your self the difficult questions that might come to be helping you discover the truth (Diamond, 2019).

Chapter 13: Testing Your Choices

Have you ever attempted to determine out in which a positive preference should lead you in advance than making the selection?

Anytime you face a desire that doesn't have a smooth solution, you may get caught for the duration of the data section at the identical time as looking at records, which needlessly prolongs the process.

There will also be a time at the same time as you could't even make a selection. Basically, you need to discover a manner to cast off "assessment paralysis" so you ought to make options quicker.

"Random" Decision Help

Some researchers from Switzerland (Douneva et al., 2019) did some experiments to find out if "random selection aids" really help speed up the method of creating picks. What are those "random desire aids?"

Well, you aren't going to just accept as actual with it, but they're coin flips. You is probably wondering that flipping a coin can assist making a decision among McDonald's and Burger King. This might be an inappropriate way to determine whether or not or not to stop your device, exchange faculties, or give up a relationship.

The examine suggests that flipping a coin may be beneficial while you need to make a few big alternatives, too. They explained that flipping a coin didn't honestly motive someone to do what the coin said. It changed into more like the flip of a coin helped them clarify what that they had already decided and have been likely going to do it besides.

This offers you a few "desire closure" to ensure that you're feeling as even though you can in the end surrender spinning your wheels at the same time as you are running thru the information phase. In concept, this can make feel, but do you've got sufficient evidence to understand for positive? Flipping a coin permit you to stay away from "evaluation paralysis" through way of getting rid of the need for information.

In one of the numerous studies the Swiss did (Douneva et al., 2019), some volunteers were assigned to a random business business enterprise. They had been then knowledgeable to read a story about someone who modified into on the brink of have a settlement renewal.

Then they needed to determine on whether or not or not or now not this individual's

settlement want to be renewed. They had been informed that they have got been handiest growing a initial choice. They need to later alternate their minds in the event that they would like to, and they could get more statistics.

The businesses had been knowledgeable that considering that a few humans have a hard time making picks, they'll use a coin to assist them make a choice. They done a virtual coin toss that might suggest transferring ahead with their first preference or suggested that they do the alternative. While these organizations have been doing this, the opposite agency become met with an hourglass that turned around and had to count on the begin of the subsequent detail.

All of the volunteers had been asked inside the occasion that they wanted greater facts earlier than carrying out the final choice. If they spoke back with "no," they had to provide them with their desire. If they stated "positive," they had been given extra records. They in the long run had to deliver them their choice.

The questions that needed to be replied have been, "What impact, if any, did the coin flip have on their records-looking for behavior?" Did a coin turn help them stick with their first desire? Did they pass on the identical time as requested inside the occasion that they preferred extra facts? Was there any kind of "evaluation paralysis" and had to gain greater statistics in advance than they might reach their closing selection?

The prevent give up end result regarded to be like what the researchers had predicted. The volunteers who flipped a coin didn't ask for more data than the possibility group did. It in truth didn't consider range how the coin become flipped. Anytime the coin turn said they should do the alternative of the selection that that they had made, it made them greater positive about the selection they had to start with made, and that they weren't as willing to ask for extra records.

This suggests that the coin flip won't be all that critical, but the real flipping of the coin and looking at their response to that coin flip can help them benefit more clarity. Take Some Action

When you locate yourself dealing with a difficult desire approximately some thing you are on foot on, see the manner you feel if you make a desire, carry out a coin flip, and notice what it lands on. See what selection you are making on the same time because the coin tells you what you have to do.

After that, perform a touch self-mirrored image. Are you glad with how the coin turn have become out? Would you need it if the coin had landed otherwise? See which eventually ends up assisting you find clarity together with your alternatives. Did it become making topics much less difficult that permits you to decide to a choice?

You are notwithstanding the truth that growing and evolving as a human every day. Any selection you are making isn't going to be set in stone besides because you'll probably determine to trade your thoughts in an afternoon, week, month, or 365 days.

Zooming In and Out

Do you apprehend how Einstein got here up with the concept of relativity? Do you recognize how Newton placed gravity? In what way did Marie Curie use radioactivity in her studies?

All of these humans used trouble-solving talents to find out the solutions to the hard problems that they have been going through. Problem-solving competencies could probable simply be the maximum powerful capability that you could very very own nowadays. If you strive to break it down, solving problems is simplest a machine to make choices on the way to bring about a way to a tough problem. This is a fluid method. It is going to be messy. It is going to take some time, however it's far constantly found in your every day lives.

Everybody has his non-public way of fixing problems, however there are a few processes which might be loads greater effective than others. My desired manner is called the Zoom Method.

- Zoom Method

This method is a manner to shift your perspective at the way you take a look at any problem. It has steps: zooming out and then zooming in. There is fee in each one. In one, you could see the larger image. On the alternative, you could see the fantastic statistics. The technique beneath will assist you discover each one.

You start with the useful aid of zooming out. Have you ever positioned yourself mesmerized by using way of the tiniest records? Focused at the smallest earlier than you in fact keep close to how huge the trouble absolutely is? If you don't make an effort to zoom out, you will find yourself caught. You are taking walks inside the timber in which you need to be searching at the entire wooded location.

So, your first step is zooming out of the trouble you're within the middle of and seeing the bigger photo. What are some subjects you are attempting to cope with? Do the ones items match into the larger scheme of existence? Is there absolutely everyone else concerned? Figure out what you are coping with and the manner it exists to the whole lot else in your international.

When you are able to try this, you are going to get a better experience of the trouble, but it can provide you with a better knowledge of the way you can approach the trouble to find out an answer. It may additionally additionally help you discover patterns, "first ideas," and give you a map of the entire hassle earlier than figuring out to take any action.

You can do that in numerous methods. It is probably as simple as zooming out to view the trouble in terms of a bigger agency. But you'll possibly zoom out traditionally so that you can get an information of the problem through time.

The way you zoom out relies upon on the cutting-edge situation, but both way, you HAVE to zoom out. It goes to have a few problems. You can also need to get stuck up for your large imaginative and prescient without facts the way you may remedy the problem. Anytime you're stuck up within the why in choice to how you need to zoom in all over again.

Once you have a address at the hassle, you can start grade by grade zooming in and knowing the information about the hassle. Once you have got the bigger photo in mind, the tiny portions will start making more feel. You will begin to see the way they wholesome collectively even as on foot with each unique. Solutions which you weren't able to see in advance than will begin to expose up.

This isn't most effective a one-time difficulty every. You want to be constantly zooming as you'll constantly be hitting roadblocks and getting stuck. Zooming is in a role to help you trade the way you consider a solution at some point of any step of the way. You need to apply it as speedy as you could and as frequently as you could.

This is in which you will discover truely how treasured zooming can be. It allow you to get a hold near at the hassle that you are going through, from a protracted way away, near up, and in every path. Having a majority of those perspectives goes to make a international of difference.

Basically, the zoom approach's fee is what forces you to count on deeper approximately any hassle which you might be managing. Too regularly, you soar right in and try to solve your issues without even understanding them. Even even though enthusiasm is a outstanding aspect, it is able to set you as a great deal as fail.

When you make an effort to assume through your troubles, have a observe and interpret them, you'll be capable of remedy them. Knowing your problem is step one to help you remedy your issues. This is likewise the maximum critical step inside the approach. Using the zoom approach will ensure that you take some time you want to find the knowledge earlier than you start appearing.

Chapter 14: Take The Three Ps

What are the maximum vital topics to don't forget at the identical time as you make a decision?

When it includes you decide, you have got the 3 Ps to maintain in thoughts. These 3 Ps are alternatives, payoffs, and opportunities. Most of the time, the ones gadgets are going to be related, and also you don't ought to examine each one in my opinion, but they may be though there if you want to do not forget.

Preferences

If a person gave you a desire among listening to Green Day or Kenny G, that could you pick? When developing a desire between together super alternatives, the thoughts is going to assign every object with a price. There is a gap inside the mind called the ventromedial prefrontal cortex (vmPFC) that works to assess the ones values and could provide you with a difference among them. The vmPFC will deliver the versions it well-knownshows to different areas of the mind so that it will then motive moves needed to advantage the choice that modified into decided on.

What is the vmPFC looking at? There is one assumption that announces that we get to a preference based totally totally on the alternatives that exist already for an alternative primarily based completely totally on beyond studies. A group of scientists determined that they have got been going to determine if the vmPFC used beyond testimonies, and in that case, how?

Their check asked their volunteers to rate how lots they preferred numerous musicians throughout numerous genres. They were then placed in a brain scanner and requested to pick out among musicians from the listing. When they made their selection, the volunteers needed to endure in thoughts the general category, which incorporates "Do I pick out jazz over pop?" But similarly they needed to consider man or woman examples. They located that the alternatives the volunteers made were biased closer to the alternatives that they had indexed in advance. The lovers of dad track ended up selecting Britney Spears or Celine Dion more regularly than they notion they may primarily based on the ratings that that they had given them.

Imaging of the mind determined that the vmPFC seems at a desire as "default minus opportunity." The essential default can be that any person from a preceding favored class and the other desire may be from each other class. The baseline hobby became greater for folks that have been a part of the popular business enterprise, which gave those alternatives a boost over the options. When human beings were requested to pick among gadgets, like magazines and food, they furnished similar outcomes. Therefore, the thoughts should use a primary method to determine on the way to help to shop time and effort, but it creates a bias.

We all have our possibilities. Understanding what your options are will can help you for your preference-making machine. Knowing your options can help manual you in lifestyles, your career, and in numerous different areas. How are you able to determine out what your options are?

First, attempt taking a examine all your reports. What sorts of jobs have you ever ever had? What matters did you take element in even as you were in faculty? What are topics which you experience doing? Look at the whole lot you've got achieved, normal jobs, volunteer paintings, and something else. Write down everything you may don't forget about the ones subjects and what you did.

For all the studies you have had, write out the property you preferred and didn't like approximately the revel in. This ought to encompass humans, duties, or exceptional memories you had. You must additionally encompass the matters which you were best at and what you weren't so unique at. Once you've got collected all of this statistics and determined a few things which you like or don't like, you may begin identifying your alternatives.

For instance, if you discovered that you favored instances at the same time as you have been on foot by myself, then a desire is probably autonomy or strolling on your very very own. You can also even take the weaknesses you determined and decide that you want to show them into options by means of the usage of manner of working on them and getting better at them.

When you have got a extra conscious concept of your opportunities, you can be more involved inside the desire-making approach in desire to allowing your thoughts to artwork on autopilot.

Payoff

When thinking about your alternatives, you may additionally ought to think about the payoff of the picks. The payoff is in fact what you could get whilst you make the choice. This is likewise referred to as Risk and

Reward. Managing risks is a few aspect we must do each day, specially at the same time as managing sports that have unsure results. Every selection you are making have to have some sort of chance that desires to be taken into consideration. The great aspect if you need to do is examine the Risk and Reward of all your alternatives in advance than making a decision (Better Decisions with Preference Theory, 2014). To help you take into account the payoff, you first need to have a observe the styles of hazard. Broadly, there are seven varieties of hazard resources:

1.Strategic – those are the dangers you look for even as developing with a plan, some aspect that is probably capable of float wrong

2.Compliance – the ones are risks that have prison or regulatory components, on the side of prison guidelines that you could spoil

3.Financial – that is any hazard that would price your coins

4.Operational – those are the maximum risks that would have an impact to your potential to execute the plan you've got were given offer you with

five.Reputational – this is any threat that might damage you as someone or your reputation

6.Other risks – monetary instability, political, natural disasters, and so forth.

7.Residual – this is any danger that remains after you've got achieved all that you could do to restriction chance

To help manipulate every of these dangers, you can take this 4-step way.

1.You should understand what the danger is. Describe how the choice may also want to negatively impact your objects.

2.You could study. This way which you may prioritize the sports based at the severity and risk of the threat to determine out the suitable stage of chance.

3. You will manage the threat. This is in which you offer you with corrective moves to help mitigate any danger that might arise.

4. You need to display screen the scenario and preserve up with the mitigation paintings.

Probability

That brings you to the ultimate P. When considering the payoff of choice, you want to reflect onconsideration on the chance that a sure very last consequences will take region based totally on the choice you made. Probability performs a big position in every location of our lives. It is a massive energy in the preference-making approach. Unfortunately, the majority humans don't have an first-rate information of opportunity. We rely on guesswork in area of calculated risks at the equal time as making selections. We permit our cognitive biases to influence the selections we make.

Smart humans are normally making stupid choices. This is in particular right with reference to gambling. While we are speakme about selections, playing is a outstanding metaphor for decision-making. To offer you with an splendid concept of the way terrible we are at calculating opportunity, I want you to keep in mind this question; "How many processes are there to set up a deck of gambling playing cards?"

The variety is probably lots bigger than you watched, so large in truth that I won't kind out all the zeros. It is 8, observed through 67 zeros, which in words is 80 unvigintillion. There are extra procedures to arrange a deck of playing cards than there are atoms inside the international.

The cause we battle with identifying the possibility of a few detail taking place is due to cognitive bias. We see patterns everywhere. That's how the thoughts works. We even generally have a tendency to find out styles in matters which may be sincerely a twist of destiny. For example, if you had been flipping a coin, and all six times it landed on heads, you will revel in that the danger that it's going to land on heads the seventh time is higher than it landing on tails. However, that's no longer the real hazard. The tendency to truly accept as real with that a future possibility is altered thru preceding occasions at the same time as in all reality, they aren't changed in any respect is what's called the Gambler's Fallacy.

So, the subsequent time you're looking at the odds that some component goes to occur after making a decision, have a take a look at the entire image and don't depend too much on preceding consequences.

Chapter 15: Get Ready To Make A Wrong Decision

Have you ever decided, and it did now not exercising consultation the least bit such as you idea it might?

You ought to possibly have heard someone allow you to recognize that it's far okay to fail and you want to fail frequently in case you would love to be successful. Being afraid of failing will keep you from the begin assignment that would lead you to success. Because you need to start in case you want to finish, and also you need to complete to be successful, being frightened of failing turns into being a self-pleasant prophecy.

It may be very obvious this concept will cowl making a few very incorrect alternatives. It isn't pretty a lot gaining knowledge of the manner to make an splendid decision and having failure appear, however you need to be organized to make a few incorrect choices. Basically, in case you aren't making incorrect choices, you aren't making sufficient choices.

Part of your adventure needs to be learning to make selections while not having all the belongings, time, and facts. It goes to take some exercising to appearance that maximum of the time, maximum of those devices don't assist making a decision except. They might probably even make it more hard to even make a selection which you need to make. Most of them offer you with extra possibilities than you have to paintings thru.

There is a large hole amongst assets, time, and records to help you determine what comes out of this tool. People who've extra revel in might be capable of bounce this hollow quicker, and typically they've got masses higher achievement. They apprehend techniques to "tuck and roll" and maintain their eyes at the prize inside the event that they make a incorrect desire.

As you start gaining momentum in your art work, you can want to make more picks because of the truth its visibility and scope increase. If you are unsure approximately the manner to make a outstanding desire and are recovering from a lousy one in case you are simply starting, it'll possibly be plenty extra hard to make the ones alternatives if human beings are looking and your alternatives have a huge impact.

If you don't have that lots experience, belongings, and thoughts-set, you have got were given got the perfect platform on which to make your incorrect selections. Do you want to make a wrong desire within the the front of just a few human beings or an entire crowd of humans?

Even even though we may not find it irresistible, we were compelled to investigate from our errors. The results of this are that we first-rate learn how to advantage achievement via making mistakes and failing.

If this is too tough, allow me try to make it a bit clearer:

- Begin a advertising and marketing marketing campaign, after which 3 months in and also you discover that it is incorrect for you

- File your taxes wrong, and your joyful day turns into a nightmare

- Give a speech in which no one listens

- Talk with any man or woman crucial, and you exceptional become looking like an fool

- Market an occasion, company, or product that no one is interested by

- Choose the incorrect partner and lose the whole lot

- Begin the usage of the incorrect tech help and characteristic all your pc systems crash

- Hire the incorrect employee, and also you want to fireside them

These aren't the exquisite snap shots, however you need to pay attention the fact in preference to it just being sugar-covered. After years of assisting human beings, I surely have found that now not telling people the unsightly truth that doesn't get shared can purpose masses greater struggling as it is easy for someone to count on all the inconvenient truths, making them sense silly or insufficient. It isn't you.

I am now not telling you that you want to make incorrect alternatives purposefully, and I'm not encouraging you to get better at making them. If it sincerely takes vicinity that you need to, be prepared to make wrong alternatives to get better at life.

A exceptional very last outcomes of this is that after you can learn how to embody that making wrong alternatives will make it much much less hard an extraordinary way to decide frequently and early. This can reduce the fatigue you feel on the same time as trying to make selections.

It may be tough to apprehend what a very good desire or a wrong choice is. What might also look precise in recent times may not look so brilliant in a month from now. Think approximately a desire you are stuck on right now. Do you need more facts, or do you just want to leap in with each feet?

What Should You Do If You Make Wrong Decisions?

Everyone goes to make a wrong preference every now and then. You understand that acquainted feeling, your belly clenches, your coronary coronary heart beats faster, and your arms get sweaty; you concept you made the right choice, but even as the effect of this feature units in, you may see that your judgment was horribly wrong (Friedlander, 2019).

You would possibly have made the selection to depart your approach for a extraordinary one, but you recognise that you chose the incorrect organization business enterprise to art work for. Maybe you broke up collectively with your partner for the duration of an issue splendid to realise which you in no way desired to depart them. Maybe you acquire that amazing red automobile you noticed, after which as you are riding it home, you get hit with purchaser's remorse.

We are all human right right here, and due to this we aren't proof in opposition to creating incorrect choices every now and then. Even no matter the fact that you could't journey once more in time to make a high-quality desire, you can reduce its effect on you. Here are some hints to help you stay on those incorrect alternatives:

1. Accept Any Emotion That Happens

It isn't going to help you in any way in case you suppress your emotions. It may be very essential which you interest on the manner you enjoy. Your first step desires to be recognizing what really occurred and the way you sense. Pretending or definitely ignoring handiest leaves the ache great open. If you with the aid of risk reduce yourself, you aren't going to fake that you don't care or it didn't appear. You are going to each bandage it your self or discover a scientific medical doctor that will help you.

If you experience like you need it, recall going to a therapist who assist you to art work thru the topics that befell. You also can communicate to a near buddy or family member that you be given as authentic with or write about it in a journal (Friedlander, 2019).

2. Focus On The Facts

After you have recognized and then general your emotions after a wrong choice, the remarkable problem you may do is consciousness on all of the data. Move a ways from the pressure and feelings and take a first-rate tough take a look at all of the statistics. Ask yourself those questions: "What is taking location right now?" "What do you virtually want?" "Are there methods you may productively artwork toward your goals in the state of affairs you're in right now?"

You may also moreover have troubles with being goal, and if that does appear, write approximately the situation. You ought to talk to a family member or friend that you take delivery of as real with to get a few exceptional individual's attitude (Friedlander, 2019).

3.Never Allow A Wrong Decision To Consume You

It can be very vital that permits you to mentally separate your self out of your choice. If you could try this, you may strip it of its power.

When you're making a incorrect choice, you generally offer it pretty a few that means that it absolutely doesn't have. You also can inform your self which you are stupid, you could't be relied on, this may ruin your dating or life, and so forth.

You should go through in mind that this isn't actual, but it'd although be difficult to move beforehand in case you get stuck with this mindset. You need to decide the instant you're making the mistake that you're going to research some factor from it after which use that as a momentum builder to help you pass in advance. If you could cast off the error's terrible meanings that you have given, you could use it to move forward and make some picks which is probably more in step with your desires.

4.Forgive

You can't be too difficult on your self in case you make a wrong choice. You ought to forgive yourself. You will usually be your very personal worst enemy that makes incorrect alternatives. You spend an excessive amount of power rolling round in guilt in desire to using it to get to our next big factor.

Use your screw ups and wrong alternatives to leverage your success. You want errors so you can be successful. Everyone goes to make mistakes, but the problem that determines your achievement is the manner you reply.

five.Accept Any Regrets

After you're making a incorrect preference, your thoughts is going to be flooded with plenty of regrets. These regrets is probably a powerful device for you. Regret ought that will help you keep in mind all of the ones subjects that you need to live a ways from in lifestyles. It also can help you're making higher selections in the future. Accept the regret and preserve moving within the direction of your dreams.

6. If Regret Consumes You, Practice Gratitude

Everyone has a few regrets. These are matters that we want we hadn't said or might have completed in a wonderful way. You can't allow these regrets manage you. You need to discover ways to manipulate mind so that you can see all of the positives in preference to the negatives.

A proper manner to peer the positives is thru the usage of gratitude. Every morning you need to make a listing of approximately five things that you are grateful for. This can help lessen remorse's grip.

7. Make a Decision-Making Process For Your Future

When you get confronted with a big preference, you could sense confused or worrying that you could make every different incorrect selection. To put off this tension, consider you decide-making way for all of your future selections.

Everybody desires to have some form of approach in location for tough picks. Hard picks are the ones with a purpose to have a large give up result and requires you to analyze various factors earlier than you are making them.

There are some steps to this option-making process:

- Find the problem; get as specific as you can

- Collect as masses records as you could that will help you make alternatives

- Think about unique answers

- Look on the proof for each feasible solution

- Make a choice

- Take the essential movement for this decision

- Look back at your choice when you have taken some movement

Now which you are armed with this manner, with a bit of success, you may be calmer now which you understand any large choices you're making on your future can be nicely concept out and nicely informed.

Chapter 16: Take A Stand

As quickly as you have got decided, learn to take a stand. It will remodel your preference into movement.

Do you want to determine out what your motive is and take a stand for a few thing? The excellent manner to determine this out is to have a have a look at the lives of others who stay cause-driven lives. We all keep in mind at the same time as Colin Kaepernick decided on to take a knee in the course of the National Anthem to make a announcement about police violence in competition to human beings of color. While you may no longer recall Kaepernick, there can be but masses to analyze from him. No don't forget what your ideals are, his actions offer us with a smooth picture of what someone with a motive looks like.

There isn't any doubt that our values shape our experience of self, which makes them an vital a part of developing with our personal emblem. Our values are our requirements or ideas of actions. It is what we view as critical in existence. Our values keep the whole thing that we want to be, what we stand for, and the way we hook up with others. There isn't always this type of thing as having the proper values or the wrong values. It's much like there isn't a right or incorrect desired taste of ice cream. Values are distinctly private and man or woman and are what make us specific. However, there can be instances at the same time as you need to check in along facet your current scenario and alter your values as a end result. There are some of critical motives why you want to determine out what your values are.

1. Values upload that means and purpose for your existence.

Figuring out what your values are and living constantly with them can be a terrific way to inject ardour, because of this, and purpose into who you are. It represents our personal goals, that is what you discover most essential. When you connect to your values, you're bringing strength and because of this into your lifestyles. When you continually communicate those items, others will understand precisely what you stand for.

2. Values provide you with a feel of achievement and nicely-being.

When you stay in congruence alongside aspect your values, it may bring about feelings of nicely-being, happiness, and success. When you stay inconsistent together together along with your values, it may become causing you to experience dissatisfied or uncomfortable, which could make you enjoy unusual.

3.Values can function one of the first-class guides.

They act as guiding necessities that permit you to pass through lifestyles, lots like a compass. If it's far pointing north, you recognize what path you're heading in and the way you may get there. It's vital to apprehend that goals and values are various subjects. Values don't want to do with the stuff you need in lifestyles however are approximately how you need to behave, behave, and relate to one-of-a-kind people alongside the way.

4.Values offer you with motivation.

Values can act as an extremely good motivator in life. They emerge as even greater critical while topics start to get hard in life and might make your struggles and difficult paintings well well well worth all the try. Furthermore, expect you word any discrepancies most of the manner you're residing your lives and your values. In that case, this will be a massive motivator to help you take dedicated motion to beautify your lives via making sure you stay more consistent with your values.

Everybody need to have some factor to face for. We want to recognize how we in shape into the large image, and we're capable of become making the arena a higher place. We need to apprehend that there can be a way that we are able to make a distinction and that there may be something that we're capable of enhance, create, or alternate to assist others.

Studies have positioned that a experience of motive is definitely one of the maximum essential indicators of happiness. Standing up for a few thing and supporting others doesn't truly help the other individual. It is also important to our normal well-being. But the caveat to this is that we must discover this cause for ourselves, and no longer because of the fact we feel that we need to or due to the truth we want to appearance terrific. We want to without a doubt surely care approximately a few element (Orban, 2019).

Figuring Out What You Stand for

How are you capable of determine out your values? There are a few notable strategies you could do this. Let's go through a few questions that permit you to. We'll moreover be the use of the Kaepernick instance right right here to help make easy some matters.

1.What are you willing to offer it all up for?

Kaepernick took a knee to offer a voice to individuals who didn't have one. In doing so, he ended up losing his pastime. He is privy to who he is, what he stands for, and in the long run, he changed into willing to lose his undertaking for it.

Take a second to keep in mind all the physical comforts which you need in lifestyles. Perhaps you want as a way to take lavish vacations, buy a larger house, or a ultramodern car. Maybe it could be some topics which may be greater modest than that. Regardless, absolutely everyone has a few bodily dreams. Imagine that inside the destiny you've got were given acquired the whole lot which you want.

Now reflect onconsideration on what you'll be willing to provide all of that up for. At first, there may not appear to be something that you might be willing to lose all of that stuff for, but all people preference some with more that means as you dig deeper. Really are trying to find inside your self to determine out what you will be inclined to offer it all up for. Once you determine that out, you may be headed towards your values and cause.

2.Where does your braveness originate?

Think approximately all of the worry that maximum dad and mom could probable revel in if we have been to transport in opposition to our u.S. Of the united states, company, business enterprise, and all at the identical time as on countrywide television. Kaepernick possibly felt some of that form of fear, however that also didn't stop him from doing what he did. He had the courage of his ideals and values to assist him overcome that.

Think approximately a second on your existence at the same time as you weren't afraid. Maybe you spoke as much as any individual or a group of human beings that you had been usually frightened of. Maybe you selected to pursue a few component that seemed to defy everything else that you as quickly as belief modified into actual. Maybe you risked emotional or physical danger knowingly for a purpose.

When we skip after some trouble this is consistent with our values, we have a tendency to lose that worry. When we connect with a few issue large than ourselves, fear is not important. When we actually apprehend what's proper, we comprehend that the fear we are experiencing is inaccurate. Figure out in which this braveness comes from, and there's a extremely good chance that your cause isn't some distance at the back of.

three. What is your coronary heart telling you?

The coronary coronary heart has 40,000 neurons that have the capacity to keep in mind, have a look at, experience, and sense matters. There is lots of strength in the heart, and it's crucial that you discover ways to tap into that strength. Think about a few aspect that calls out to you from deep interior your soul. What have you let the mind speak you out of, in spite of the truth that deep down you really wanted to do it? You had possibly heard this while you had been showering at the same time as taking a relaxing stroll or at the equal time as the usage of. When you are taking a harm from life, what is it that bubbles up on your thoughts?

You spend a whole lot of a while taking note of your thoughts, but it is the coronary heart that has the first rate answers. What receives your coronary coronary heart pumping, fills you with pleasure, or makes it skip a beat?

Maybe you become feeling every other person's ache and understand that you could assist them in some way. When you've got a study your coronary heart, you could find out your values.

There are a number of human beings inside the global who can permit you to recognize what they will be closer to. However, you want to take a awesome stance. Instead of telling every person what you hate, try reputation up for the subjects which you accept as true with in. Everybody is right right here for a few component that is large than

you.

You need to additionally test your values in numerous areas of your existence, like fitness, network, social relationships, circle of relatives relationships, and artwork. Think approximately the way you would love to exude your non-public logo throughout these numerous domains, then discover the numerous techniques wherein you could live in more congruence with the values of these domain names.

Of route, all of this mirrored image goes to require that you set apart some time for private mirrored image. However, what you could revel in in lifestyles after this is going to be well without a doubt well worth it.

When you enjoy loneliness and ache, this is due to the disconnection you're experiencing out of your reason. There can be human beings reachable a wonderful manner to be important of your stance, but that doesn't endorse you are incorrect or that you need to alternate what you believe in.

Chapter 17: Don't Beat Around The Bush

Take a second to anticipate that you are sitting stuffed in an overcrowded subway automobile within the center of a warmth wave in August without a aircon. You see someone approximately three seats from you attain his hand out and grabs the butt of a female recognition in front of him. She yelps, takes more than one steps from him and is manifestly dissatisfied. Nobody else appears to have observed or cares. Do you sit there, like everybody else, or do you speak up?

If that one turn out to be too immoderate, let's do this one on for length. You have located that a person you parent with, regarded to be your boss's protégé, has been skimming cash from the organisation for non-public use. However, you don't recognise the brilliant way to supply this as much as the boss because of the reality you're concerned that you could be seen as a tattle tale.

Are you going to talk up, or do you maintain the call of the game to yourself?

Plenty human beings have a first rate idea of what sort of human beings select out to take some shape of motion in the ones kinds of conditions. Forceful, most possibly. Somebody who is used to taking rate in situations. A individual who has a completely strong moral compass. Unsure? Shy? Probably now not.

However, the studies into which character chooses to interfere in those types of conditions virtually receives rid of these assumptions and can mean that internalizing those devices can also want to suggest that they pass over out on a remarkable exchange to assist someone. It is real that the passive bystander has a dishonest to outnumber the energetic ones, however studies have decided that folks who pick out out out to say a few difficulty have a tendency no longer to be that one-of-a-kind, person-sensible, from anybody else.

It doesn't suggest that they are constantly greater bold or outgoing than everybody else with a median character. Philip Zimbardo and Zeon Franco, psychologists, have spoken approximately "the banality of heroism," arguing that almost everyone reachable have to grow to be intervening to help other human beings. The lively bystander usually comes with unique trends, but the ones functions don't come from their innate nature. There are a number of characteristics that human beings can grow to be gaining knowledge of inside the event that they want to.

To assist domesticate those capabilities, you will need to undergo a piece of education or training that teaches you to need to revel in assured while a second requires them to obtain this. Secondly, do have a presence of thoughts to choose the great form of response that strains up with what you consider in, which sees others as deserving help regardless of what.

The detail that has a tendency to set those interveners aside from others is "self-efficacy." This method they consider themselves to tackle a few form of movement a good way to be beneficial in some way. This self perception may additionally come from having stepped in on similar moments, however it could come from practice and schooling.

While it's no longer possible to duplicate a success intervention evaluations, there are efforts that you could take that provide you with a hazard to exercise this in faux conditions. That's whilst Lynne Henderson, a psychologist, and representative Brooke Deterline, got right down to create a practice consultation-type method so as to assist human beings to cultivate the talents they need to have the self perception to speak up for matters they acquire as right with in. This cognitive-behavioral-based totally training posits that everybody, irrespective of how withdrawn or shy he may be, is able to examine the manner he can assert himself via taking the time to exercise it in precise situations until this form of interaction turns into second nature. When you think about telling your boss approximately your coworker's wrongdoing, a hurry of pressure chemical compounds is sent inside the path of your body, looking for to get you to live quiet.

But, you may use exercise versions of this shape of state of affairs so you can get acquainted with that rush of stress chemical substances and get used to it sufficient to speak up in spite of these chemical compounds. That will assist you building up the self notion to intervene in advantageous conditions regardless of the reality which you are experiencing worry. After deliberate exercising, Henderson's application, like many others, gave humans the equipment favored to talk out in stressful moments, much like the education that medical doctors get hold of. In the put up-education checks, the individuals cautioned feeling an awful lot much less anxious and annoying at the same time as it got here to maintaining themselves than they did in advance than.

Courage When Needed

In this social flight simulation application, the aim is to get your self equipped to call upon all the assertiveness that you want while you want it, mainly if it's no longer the form of person you generally are. If you are obviously introverted, you might not be able to see yourself screaming, "STOP," so loud it echoes all through the subway.

But on the equal time as you make the effort to rehearse the ones conditions or comparable ones, you'd possibly revel in bolder. Besides feeling as although you're equipped for the project reachable, maximum interveners can have a massive circle of problem this is bigger than their family and buddies, that's a awesome that you'll want to domesticate.

We're going to take a trouble-step for a 2d and communicate about worry. Have you ever taken a moment to consider what you outline worry as? The dictionary tells us that worry is "an ugly emotion due to the perception that a person or some thing is risky, in all likelihood to cause ache or a chance."

Sure, that is probably what fear does to someone bodily and mentally, however that doesn't propose that's in which fear stops. Fear can also serve as a danger for self-boom and self-discovery. It can characteristic a nicely of untapped strength and power. Fear sucks; I acquired't deny that. There are also some of existence-threatening situations and instances that purpose quite some worry that I desire no person ever needed to experience.

But there is moreover every other spectrum of fear that originates internal us and is regularly due to our very very own self esteem. This is the concern that has a tendency to keep someone lower again from residing an adequate life. To upward thrust up for what you trust in, you have to discover ways to address that fear. You ought to observe that your fear does no longer outline you and that you could release it (How to Stand Up for What's Right, Even If You're Afraid, n.D.).

The reality of the trouble is, fear has an inclination to be gift on a everyday foundation for most parents, however the manner it makes a decision to present itself is constantly converting. You could in all likelihood revel in uncertainty, lack of motivation, confusion, a deep anxiety, tension, or some aspect that you could't call deep internal you. There is a super hazard which you have skilled fear on severa special degrees and in unique forms. Aside from taking a category that teaches you the manner to get up for subjects, there are techniques that you may flip that fear you are experiencing into power. Let's skip over four steps to reworking your worry (How to Stand Up for What's Right, Even If You're Afraid, n.D.).

1.Take some time for remarkable self-speak and self-reflected picture.

The next time you begin to experience uncertain, afraid, stressful, or annoying, I want you to dig deep and find out what lies underneath the ones feelings. Are you tense about making use of for a project due to the fact you're afraid that they may say no? If they don't lease you, does that sincerely recommend which you aren't pinnacle sufficient and received't enjoy career fulfillment? You apprehend that's no longer proper, but it's far a very common manner to take pleasure in unstable self-speak. Most of the time, it's miles all about wondering that you aren't really worth enough to enjoy success or happiness.

You want to be sincere with yourself and decide out the foundation of the worry you're experiencing. Take the awful announcement you bought here up with and rewrite it to make an empowering declaration that tells you the opportunity of your proscribing belief.

2.Weigh all of your options.

Still don't comprehend if it might be properly well worth your at the equal time as to stand up for some issue; have a take a look at the specialists and cons of each. Would you as an alternative stand up for what you take delivery of as authentic with in and pursue your imaginative and prescient and ardour? Or do you need to really preserve the repute quo? You will probably come to recognize that there are more experts to overcoming your fears than actually sticking with the recognition quo.

3.Take steps to behave.

All of the arrows are pointing inside the right direction in case you want to take a stand. Yes, it's miles possible to act inside the face of your fears whilst now not having to fear approximately the entire worldwide crashing spherical you. The next issue you need to do is virtually do it. Take a stand for some element. That very first step you're taking inside the right route toward your values is probably a large one. Yes, it's also the toughest step you'll need to take. Remember, it is first rate in case you take smaller steps on the begin. You don't should jump head first into some component. Small steps and status up for topics, even within the smallest techniques, allow you to learn how to cope with the ones emotions of worry.

4.Reward your self when you have confronted your fears.

When you communicate, intervene, or arise for some aspect in a few fashion no matter the fact which you were afraid to achieve this, supply yourself a pat at the lower again. Reward yourself for performing some component applicable. This goes to feed that wonderful momentum and keep you walking toward more top notch subjects and taking stands.

The super problem approximately following the ones four steps is that whenever you make a decision to look beneath the ground and simply figure out what is causing your worry, you can get closer to running together along with your personal electricity and turning into extra aligned with who you're and what you would love your life to be. It is likewise going to get simpler the more frequently you do it.

One have a take a look at has determined that this kind of good sized undertaking about others facilitates to act due to the reality the gasoline for a number of interventions. You are probably going to experience skittish about repute up for a few other man or woman or your mind. However, introverts and extroverts alike have the capacity to interfere at the identical time because the time calls for it. They definitely want to discover ways to gain this.

Chapter 18: Be The Change

Right now, everywhere in the global, people are giving different humans recommendation at the manner we need to stay our lives. If we aren't giving the speech, we are writing it, education it, converting it, and then disturbing approximately it. On this route, we're studying terms, getting rid of sections, and filling it entire of sugary rubbish.

When a person says: "Welcome to the sector," what does this absolutely suggest? You had been in this worldwide for a positive quantity of years, and you may see more of it. What about the word: "New doors are beginning?" This makes a splendid fortune cookie, but you have opened and closed doors for many years now. Okay, "Go make a distinction inside the international." This is the most volatile manner to anticipate to be had. It is a recipe for a very depressing life. The next six phrases you study you need to take into account: "Don't try to change the area."

- Ego's Triumph

We have too many people searching out to alternate the arena, and I thanks. But I am not sure they may be doing it for all the proper motives. You can't inform that they are critical about it via the usage of the careers that they've decided on. I went to university for journalism, and as soon as I changed into going for walks as a journalist, I met many journalism university students. The fundamental question I got requested modified into why I went into journalism. My answer emerge as normally, "I want to make the arena a better region."

I minored in political idea, and I mingled with numerous people who actually were given into politics. They worked as campaigners, bureaucrats, or maybe a few candidates. "I want to make the arena a better vicinity." Anytime some are looking for energy and want to exchange the arena into what they assume it want to be, you want to be cautious. Some of these human beings will get into education with the notion of supporting instill the subsequent generation with new values. They would like to alternate the vicinity, too.

There are exceptional examples, and I am no longer deciding on on the ones careers via the use of any way. Let's get actual for a few minutes. Look at one small a part of the planet you have got were given been to and the tiny percent of the human beings you have got met. Your opinions are going to be skewed and limited in several procedures. Our brains have a coping mechanism on the way to idiot us into wondering that we've got were given a draw close on sincerely how massive this planet actually is. There have handiest been 12 humans who've in reality stepped onto the moon. They checked out this huge, muddy, wet ball of magma that has a crunchy shell. Those fortunate astronauts have a totally specific mind-set approximately this worldwide. People who've flown in an plane don't have a clue.

Our minds will stay constant on our horizons and are limited to what we've visible because the belief of all the unseen and unexplained is extraordinarily scary. You understand masses about the sector which you stay in thoroughly. You are a bit of it. Take your restricted revel in and pledge to apply it as a template to alternate the arena, as this will exercise your ego.

- Goals That Are Attainable

When you area a goal to alternate the region, it is exceptional going to make you depressing. Name one individual who, to you, has changed the region, and you will discover a number of pain, suffering, and now not a extraordinary deal success. You are going to find out that maximum of them died in advance than all of the topics they contributed made a distinction. You are going to find out many that have been made a laugh of for this concept. Some have been even tortured, persecuted, and killed for his or her ideals.

There is some component not unusual in the humans who've truely changed the area. They didn't set it as a aim. Their historical declare occurred as an twist of fate or a by-product of performing some thing that emerge as honestly regular. Anybody who wants to "exchange the arena" received't have the staying power to stare at the stars as Galileo did. He obtained't track the sun's moves like the Mayan calendar's creators did. He didn't mess around with chemical compounds as gunpowder's inventors did. He didn't play with moldy bread and discover penicillin. He received't have the staying strength to take a look at tiny bugs. He won't spend the time reading engineering, technological understanding, medicinal drug, and math to locate something an splendid manner to exchange the area.

People who observe medicinal drug, engineering, technological know-how, and math didn't begin with converting the arena in thoughts. They started out with the cause of helping others remedy precise troubles.

- Revolution's Business

Trying to alternate the arena is noble and one that is difficult to criticize. If you aren't snug expertise what I need to say, you want to put together yourself to get loads more uncomfortable. Most of you have got got expressed at a while or terrific that goals approximately "changing the area" have made amusing of others who they experience are "egocentric" or "grasping" for studying finance or industrial agency. In this beauty, there are human beings who have decided that tremendous humans don't have any morals due to the truth they forget about approximately the arena's problems.

But it's miles the ones business folks that make a huge distinction in the world by means of way of giving specific people possibilities. They supply services or products that boost the usual of dwelling. They rent many those who get to do what they love. What about those folks that make hundreds of masses that wind up being a philanthropist? Somebody paid for a measles vaccine to be made and disbursed all in the route of Africa. People like Warren Buffett and Bill Gates are the use of their coins to make massive versions in humans's lives, and at no time in their lifestyles did they ever say: "Hey, I want to change the arena. Let me begin by using manner of losing out of Harvard and writing an operating device for a pc."

www.ingramcontent.com/pod-product-compliance
Lightning Source LLC
Chambersburg PA
CBHW050404120526
44590CB00015B/1819